ALL OUR FUTURE

ALL OUR FUTURE

A Longitudinal Study of Secondary Education

J. W. B. Douglas
author of 'The Home and the School'
J. M. Ross and H. R. Simpson

PETER DAVIES : LONDON

Printed in Great Britain by
Morrison and Gibb Ltd,
London and Edinburgh

*To the National Survey Boys and Girls
and their Mothers who by their generous help
have made this study possible*

Acknowledgments

This study owes its success to the generous help given by Education Officers, Medical Officers of Health, teachers, school doctors and school nurses throughout the country. During the years covered by this book, it was supported by grants from the Nuffield Foundation, the Ford Foundation and the Population Council, Inc. It is now housed at the London School of Economics and is supported by the Medical Research Council as part of the Unit for the Study of Environmental Factors in Mental and Physical Illness.

Many present and past members of this Unit have helped with parts of this Study. Dr I. B. Pless has identified members of the Survey who have had a heavy load of illness and has written about their educational progress in Chapter XXIII. Dr J. E. Cooper was closely concerned with the Chapter on handedness, Dr Annette Lawson collected extra information on the broken families and Dr D. G. Mulligan was responsible for the initial work on delinquency and the behaviour ratings; Dr A. J. Costello, Mr D. M. Nelson and Mr R. K. Turner have read and commented on the manuscript; Mr I. W. Henry, Mrs Barbara Alderman and Mrs Mary Bajona have helped with the analysis; Miss Sara Excell, Mrs Charlotte Morrish, Mrs Margaret Nixon, Miss Eileen Pollard, Miss Rosa-Jane Raynham and Mrs Rita Whiting did the secretarial work.

Throughout the study, the National Foundation of Educational Research has advised us in the choice of tests and standardized them for us. We should like to thank Mr D. A. Pidgeon, who describes the fifteen year tests in Appendix I for his help; Dr W. A. Hammond has given us great help on certain aspects of the study and we have also had the benefit of advice from Professor J. Tizard and Professor A. Sorsby.

[vii]

This study would have perished many years ago if it had not been for the support of the Population Investigation Committee and we wish to express our indebtedness to them and, in particular, to Professor D. V. Glass who has, at each stage of the study, given us the benefit of his advice and criticism.

Contents

[ix]

Foreword

Each year more pupils voluntarily stay on at school past the minimum leaving age, the number sitting the General Certificate Examinations increases and the sixth forms enlarge. This expansion of education has however not so far taken quite the form expected. When the 1944 Education Act came into force giving free secondary education for all, it would have been reasonable to anticipate that the children of manual working class parents would benefit most from the increased opportunities, since previously there had been relatively few free or scholarship grammar school places available. The expressed intention of the Act was to give each child, irrespective of his family circumstances and social origins, the type of secondary education that was best suited to his abilities. Entry to any type of secondary school was not meant to be competitive—each pupil was to be allocated to the school that provided the course most appropriate to his ability. This, however, as is well known, has not been the outcome. The combination of tests, reports, examinations and interviews, which was to assess the intelligence and attainment of pupils so that they might be channelled to the most appropriate secondary schools has become a competitive examination which is a source of envy and discontent.

The demand for academic courses has increased to an unforeseen extent, and the number of successful G.C.E. candidates at all levels and in all subjects has risen more rapidly than anyone could have anticipated in 1944. That it is not only those picked out as promising pupils at eleven who succeed on academic courses is shown by the remarkable success of some independent or fee-paying schools in preparing, for 'A' levels and the universities, pupils who in the local authority 11 + selection examinations were not deemed suitable for or capable of profiting from a grammar school education; and a similar conclusion is to be drawn from the increasing number of

[xi]

secondary modern school pupils who sit 'O' levels and sometimes 'A' levels. This made the system of selection look over-restrictive and therefore wasteful of talent. This is one of the strong arguments in favour of changing to a fully comprehensive system.

The average length of school life has increased for pupils from all sections of the population. More enter the sixth form and more go on to higher education, but the additional recruits do not come wholly, or mainly, from the poorer families who would have been expected to gain most from the general expansion of opportunity.

We show in this book that in the population as a whole, as well as in the selective schools, the middle class pupils have retained, almost intact, their historic advantage over the manual working class. This was also the conclusion reached by the Committee on Higher Education (1963) from the results of a special study of school leaving age in 1961. In terms of the proportion of children getting five or more 'O' levels there has been little reduction in the differences between the social classes since the Early Leaving Report (Central Advisory Council for Education, 1954). The Committee also found in the universities that the relative proportions of students from middle and manual working class homes were the same in 1960 as in the period from 1928–47.

In other fields also it has been observed that social class differences persist, or may even increase, during a period when there is a general improvement in facilities. The infant death rate for example has declined in all social classes, but the relative difference between the the mortality of infants in the various social classes is as great today as it was 50 years ago (Morris and Heady, 1955). Indeed, if the infant mortality of clerks is compared with that of miners the difference is greater than in the past, and this in spite of the fact that the relative wage differential between these two occupations has diminished.

Another instance is the provision of maternity beds. Between 1946 and 1958 many additional beds were provided which it was hoped would be used by the women who ran the greatest risk, namely those having their first and those having their fourth or later babies. It turned out however that these additional beds were used for the most part by women having their first, second and third babies, while those having their fourth or later were no more likely to be delivered in hospital in 1958 than in 1946 (Butler and Bonham, 1963;

[xii]

Joint Committee, 1948). Thus an important and vulnerable group of women was not getting the benefits of a measure that was intended to help them. Indeed, compared with the other women, they were relatively more at a disadvantage than if the additional beds had not been provided.

Other examples could be quoted to show that in spite of the expansion of services certain groups in the population fail to benefit, or even become increasingly deprived. It is important to be aware of this possibility in education, where parents need both knowledge and intelligence if their children are to make full use of the available opportunities. As educational requirements become increasingly complex, trainings more skilled and specialized, and competition for university places more intense, so there is a danger that the pupils with less interested, less intelligent and less determined parents will fall further away from the main channel. This is a danger that can only be avoided if we know how the educational services are being used. Unfortunately official statistics, though they give accurate information for the whole country which cannot be matched by any sample study, provide for the most part isolated demographic facts which are not anchored to individual pupils and so cannot be used to show which groups in the community are failing to benefit from the services provided. It is here that the follow up of relatively small groups of pupils through the schools may provide an answer.

Nearly 20 years ago, when this study was primarily concerned with the maternity services, it was pointed out that a series of similar follow up studies spaced 10 to 15 years apart would show how the maternity services could be adjusted to meet the changing needs of mothers and children (Joint Committee, 1948). Equally such a series could be used to show how far the educational services provided were being used by the various sections of the community. In education particularly, the study of successive cohorts would show not only which families were unable or unwilling to make full use of the opportunities provided, but also at which stage such failures occur. Used in this limited way cohort studies provide a cheap method of gathering data, though in a rapidly changing society it may prove difficult to ensure that comparable information is gathered in successive studies.

We hope that this survey, which describes the educational opportunities of a generation of young people who have recently left school, will be the first of a series that will show the effects of new educational policies—their strong points as well as their weak points—by permitting direct comparisons between similar groups of pupils who have passed through the schools at intervals of say 10 to 15 years.

Disraeli once said that on the education of the people of this country its future depended and it is in this sense that we have entitled our report 'Half Our Future'.* In this sense also we have called this book—which describes the education of a representative sample of pupils in England, Wales and Scotland—'All Our Future'.

* *Half Our Future*, Her Majesty's Stationery Office, 1963.

Part I

The National Survey

Chapter One

The Background of this Study

This book describes the progress of a group of boys and girls from the time they entered their secondary schools until they were sixteen and a half years old, by which age more than half of them had finished their formal education and most of those who were going to take the General Certificate of Education Ordinary level examinations had done so. *The Home and the School* (Douglas, 1964) described their progress through the primary schools; the present book covers the next 5 years, and further publications are planned to follow the same boys and girls into the sixth forms, higher education and employment. Scottish pupils were excluded from the earlier book since the fact that selection takes place one year later in the North made comparisons up to eleven years difficult; they are however included here. This allows us to make a number of comparisons between pupils in Scotland and the South which add to our knowledge of the effects of selection and of the limitations of some of the tests that were used. For convenience we have used the English educational terminology throughout.

The Home and the School reported on the primary school years and the 11+ selection examinations, and raised serious questions about how far children from economically or culturally deprived homes were being given the educational support they needed; they seemed to be saddled with a cumulative series of educational handicaps. Not only did they come from homes where education itself is little valued, but they were also at a disadvantage at school. Many primary schools stream their pupils at the age of seven or eight by attainment in reading and sometimes by intelligence, but assessments at this early age are far from reliable and tend to underrate in

[3]

particular the ability of the boys and girls from poor homes. Errors of placement can of course be corrected by later transfers—between streams or classes—of those who turn out to be either more or less able than expected. In fact however such transfers were rare and, when they did take place, reinforced the original social bias against the boys and girls from the poorer homes. As they grew older, pupils in each stream increasingly conformed to the earlier assessments of their ability; those in the top stream improved in tests of ability and attainment and those in the lower stream fell behind.

It is probable that these changes were a result of streaming rather than an indication of the soundness of the original assessments. The earlier predictions were constantly being reinforced in the class-rooms and probably also in the home, and so were self-fulfilling. The pupils came to set their sights and to assess their own ability according to the expectations of parents and teachers. This sorting out by ability, which started for many children in this sample during their first few years at school, became overt at the point of transfer to secondary school, at eleven in England and Wales and at twelve in Scotland.

The majority of boys and girls in this national study sat the selection examinations and on the results were allocated to grammar, technical or secondary modern schools in England and Wales and to five- or three-year courses at senior or junior secondary schools in Scotland.

Although the 11 + examinations are efficient, they are not free from social bias. When selecting in the 11 + examinations on a wide spectrum of tests, examinations and teachers' reports, it is inevitable that there should be a borderline group who, given another opportunity, might well have been allocated to different schools; within this group it was shown that those with educationally ambitious parents or at primary schools which had a good past record of getting their pupils into grammar schools were at an advantage.

A fair selection process requires that the provision of maintained secondary school places throughout the country should be closely related to the ability of the boys and girls in each locality. This was not so during the years covered by this Survey; the proportion of grammar school places available differed greatly from one local education authority to another and bore little relation to the measured ability of the pupils living in each area or to the availability of places in direct grant and independent schools.* Indeed, unless sufficient grammar-type courses in secondary modern schools are provided to offset local deficiencies in selective places, the unequal distribution of grammar school places can only lead to unequal educational opportunity. While much of the discrepancy in grammar school provision originates in local educational history, the policy in a few areas has been to keep the number of places low so as to ensure that there will be sufficient pupils in the secondary modern schools to provide academic streams of a viable size. As Peterson (1965, p. 161)† says, these authorities have 'partially solved one difficulty by negating the whole principle on which selection at eleven had been based'.

Our general impression on looking back at the primary school education of this group of boys and girls is of unequal opportunities stemming from deficiencies in the homes and the schools, and from the illogical and patchy distribution of grammar and technical school places. Now that the members of this Survey have all left their secondary schools these earlier impressions can be re-examined. How far have our gloomy predictions been justified? And how far have the environmental influences acting on the development of the boys and girls at the first stage of their school careers been reinforced or attenuated by those acting at the next?

In the present climate of educational opinion, with the imminent prospect of a wholly comprehensive system, it might be thought that the problems of selection lie in the past. If so, it is the very recent past, since even in 1965, of the 126 members of this national sample of boys and girls who had not yet entered employment or higher education, 93 were at selective schools and 33 were studying for 'O', 'A' and 'S' levels in colleges of further education, technical colleges or with tutors—there were none at comprehensive schools.

The description of the effects of selection on educational opportunity is of more than historic interest. It has relevance to the comprehensive system which is now being built up and underlines

* To avoid repetition, 'grammar', 'direct grant' and 'secondary modern' schools, unless otherwise specified, include Scottish senior secondary, grant aided and junior secondary schools respectively.
† The full reference will be found on page 231.

[5]

the dangers and consequences of hidden selection which may turn out to be more damaging than formal selection, as it lacks both the safeguards of standardized tests or examinations and the opportunities for review and revision.

It would have been a useful and interesting exercise to compare the performance of pupils in comprehensive schools with that of pupils in the selective system, but the necessary information is not to be obtained from the present study. Few of the Survey members went to comprehensive schools at eleven years, and most of these schools were little different from secondary modern schools with an academic stream. Other comprehensive schools were suffering from the counter-attractions of grammar and direct grant schools, which lured away the most able pupils and so deprived the comprehensive schools of the stimulus of a fully representative and effective sixth form.

This book is far from being solely a study of selective education and its consequences, for one of the advantages of a longitudinal study is that material collected from many different sources and at many different ages may be linked. Thus, the medical descriptions of the boys and girls are related to their school progress, as also are their family circumstances, behaviour and the complicated inter-relationships of order of birth, birth spacing and the sex of the other children in the family. We have in this way tried to take full advantage of the unique opportunities offered by this long-term study. Another study (Pringle, Butler and Davie, 1966) based on children born in the first week of March 1958 should in time allow interesting comparisons to be made with the present data.

Our aim has been to make this a non-technical book so far as is possible, though we are aware that it is difficult to satisfy both the general reader and the expert. For some there will be too little information and supporting data while for others there will be too much. A few diagrams illustrate this text, and the tables referred to in the footnotes will be found in Appendix V. The inquiring reader is also referred to fuller and more detailed tables lodged at the libraries listed at the beginning of this appendix and also to the articles listed on pages 232 to 235.

Some may wish to know what importance to give to the various differences in test scores; this necessarily will depend on the size of

[6]

the groups that are compared. With large numbers even a small difference of 0·5 points may be statistically significant—or meaningful—though not necessarily important. A substantial difference would be 2 points of test score. An increase of this amount, i.e. 2 points, in the average test performance of the pupils at eleven years for example would increase by one-quarter the numbers who would have qualified—on existing standards—for entry to grammar, direct grant or technical schools.

This book is in general concerned only with differences in test scores and percentages that are statistically significant. The importance of differences, whatever their size, is of course enhanced if they hold for a succession of measures and if all differences point in the same direction. Chapter XXI shows, for example, many consistent differences in test performance, attitudes and family background between short-sighted and normally sighted boys and girls.

This book continues the story of the boys and girls in the National Survey from the point at which they were left in *The Home and the School*. It follows them to the threshold of the sixth form and examines a number of new topics which will be of interest to those working in the general field of education and outside.

We are still in touch with these young men and women, whether they are in higher education, at work, unemployed or ill. In time we will be able to supplement the description of their school education with an account of their training within industry and the universities, technical colleges and colleges of education. We should also be able to judge how far ability and type of employment are matched. Some 400 of the men and women in this study began degree courses at home and abroad: we have been able to arrange to meet just over 200 of them in small groups. Some comments from these discussions are used in this book.

Chapter Two

Details of the Pupils

The origins of the National Survey of Health and Development are described in *The Home and the School*, and will only be briefly summarized here. The 5,362 young people in this sample were selected from all those born in Great Britain in the first week of March 1946. Illegitimate and twin births were excluded and, from the remaining legitimate single births, all middle class and all agricultural workers' children were taken but only 1 in 4 of the other manual workers' children. The sample is therefore overloaded with those from middle class families.

This has the advantage for the Survey study that appreciably more have gone on to higher education (approximately one and a half times) than would be expected from a random sample of the same size. A minor disadvantage is that, when giving descriptions that are intended to refer to the whole population, it is necessary to adjust for this sampling. To do so, all that is necessary is to give a weight of 1 to the middle class and agricultural workers' families and a weight of 4 to the remainder. The resulting rates or 'population estimates' for grammar school admissions, age of leaving school, 'O' level results, etc. lie close to known national figures, and there is every reason to believe that, when adjusted in this way, the observations made during this Survey give a true picture of the educational experience of the national age group of pupils which this sample is intended to represent.

Death and emigration have removed some of the boys and girls originally included in this study; the balance sheet* shows that in 1962, when they were sixteen and a half years of age, 4,720 were

* See Table 1.

still alive and thought to be residing in Great Britain. Some educational information, at a minimum age of leaving school and General Certificate of Education 'O' level examination results, is available for 98 per cent of these pupils, and it is probable that some of the missing 2 per cent have left the country and so should not be included.

As these young people are scattered thinly over the whole of England, Wales and Scotland, we have not tried to see them ourselves or bring them together for testing or observation. We have relied on school heads and teachers,* school doctors and nurses, health visitors, parents and the Survey members for information. It was only at a later stage that it was feasible to meet a few of them in the universities.

Tests of intelligence and attainment were given, under the supervision of a member of the school staff, to these pupils when they were eight, eleven and fifteen years, and at thirteen and fifteen years the class teachers rated them for a large number of items of behaviour, both in the class-room and outside. These behaviour ratings have been used to assess attitudes to work and to identify those pupils who, in the view of their teachers, were troublesome, nervous or aggressive. They are amplified at thirteen years by the results of a self-rating inventory, designed to assess neuroticism and the degree of introversion or extraversion. At thirteen and fifteen the pupils recorded their job hopes and aspirations for further education, their main interests, clubs and hobbies.

The age at which these pupils left school and the results of any public examinations which they sat were given to us by the headmasters and headmistresses, who also supplied information about their schools—the number and qualifications of the teaching staff, details of the school buildings, site facilities and amenities.

The school doctors, who had already examined the boys and girls when they were six, seven and eleven years, gave them a fourth special examination when they were fifteen, which took approximately one hour to complete. This included a description of their secondary sexual characteristics, which was used to assess the boys' stage of puberty. The school nurses or health visitors, who had called at the homes and interviewed the parents on many occasions,

* We have used the term 'teachers' throughout this book instead of 'masters' or 'mistresses'.

[9]

also made one further visit when the pupils were fifteen years. In addition to bringing information up to date on home circumstances, health and symptoms such as bed-wetting, unexplained abdominal pain and vomiting, they asked the parents about their hopes and aspirations for the future employment and training of their sons and daughters. For the first time information was gathered on the health of both parents and the mothers completed a shortened version of the Maudsley Personality Inventory.* A time-table showing the ages at which different types of information were collected is shown in Appendix II.

Although the results of the G.C.E. 'O' level examinations and the dates of leaving school are known for 98 per cent of the 4,720 Survey members living in Great Britain in 1961, full test results are available for considerably fewer; 1,094 failed to attend for testing on one or more of the three occasions. They include those withdrawn temporarily or permanently from the study, those at unco-operative schools and those who, owing to illness, temporary absence or lack of up-to-date information about their whereabouts were not able to sit some of the tests. There is no test information at all for 337 pupils, but for 757 the result of at least one group of tests is available. In other words, there is some test information for 93 per cent of the pupils living in Great Britain and full test information for 77 per cent (3,626 pupils). The latter, the educational sample, is the group used when test scores are discussed and when comparisons are made of educational performance at different ages.

It is important to know how far this fully tested group can be regarded as typical of all the boys and girls in the Survey. A detailed comparison has been made between those with full test information —'the educational sample'—and the complete sample, whether tested or not.† The educational sample contains rather fewer middle class and rather more manual working class pupils than the complete sample, but only slightly so—the social class of these young people is not significantly different from that expected, if we had taken all the 4,720 families living in Great Britain and drawn the educational sample from them at random.

The average scores for the ability and attainment tests are a little

* See Glossary page 192.
† See Table 2.

[10]

higher in the educational than in the complete sample; this holds at each age, but is greatest at eight years.* If the sample has been drawn at random from all those tested, the eight-year test scores would have been 0·3 points lower for the boys and 0·2 points lower for the girls, a small and not statistically significant difference which is partly explained by the lack of full test information for those who were semi-literate, some of whom, having sat the eight-year tests, were later transferred to special schools or streams and were considered to have insufficient educational skills to complete the subsequent written tests.

The pupils in the educational sample also do slightly better than would be expected in the G.C.E. examinations; rather more get 'good'† certificates and fewer get none, whereas the school leaving ages of the educational sample, possibly owing to the slight depletion of upper middle class families, are rather lower than expected. For both 'O' level results and pattern of leaving however the figures for the educational sample are not significantly different from those that would have been expected from a random selection from the complete sample.

The main deficiency in the educational sample lies in the disappointing response of the independent schools to our request for test information. While 86 per cent of those at independent schools were tested on at least one occasion, complete test information exists for only 45 per cent of the boys and 54 per cent of the girls. The losses are spread fairly evenly between the so-called 'public' or Headmasters' Conference schools and the other fee-paying schools. The independent school staff were rather less able or less willing than the maintained school staff to spare the time to test their pupils. Owing to this heavy loss, we have in general included pupils at independent schools with those at grammar and direct grant. The independent schools however play such an important part in the later stages of our educational system, that a rough assessment of the progress and attainment of all their pupils has been made in Chapter VIII on the basis of the test information that is available.

Apart from losses a potential source of distortion is that, as these pupils have been kept under observation for many years, there is a

* See Table 3.
† See Glossary.

[11]

general awareness that they have been picked for special study. This may have provided an incentive for them to work hard and for their parents and teachers to take a special interest in their school progress. Moreover they sat a number of tests which other pupils did not take—and in doing so may have acquired an additional facility in dealing with tests, which could have helped them when they took the 11+ selection examinations. The possibilities of distortion of this type were recognized early in this study, and one-third of the manual working class boys and girls who had been excluded from the follow-up study was set aside as a control group, against which the main Survey sample could be compared. The children in this group have been seen once only, when the school doctors gave them a special medical examination at eleven years and the school nurses called at their homes. In addition, information on the results of the secondary selection examinations, G.C.E. examinations and the age of school leaving was provided by the local education authorities. At the age of eleven, as reported in *The Home and the School*, there was little to suggest that the control group was in any way different from the main Survey sample. Similar proportions had reached grammar school and the only advantage that the pupils in the main Survey had over the controls was that they were more likely to be treated for minor eye and speech defects; in both groups however similar proportions with serious defects had been treated.

In the secondary schools rather more of the control group got good 'O' level certificates, but more in the educational sample stayed at school until the end of the 1961/2 session. These are small differences going in opposite directions and suggest that up to the age of sixteen at any rate the educational progress of the pupils in the main Survey sample has not been influenced by the additional attention they have received or the extra tests they have taken.

Part II

The Educational Process

Chapter Three

Trends in Ability and Attainment

This section of the book is concerned with the influence of secondary selection on educational opportunity and achievement: the first three chapters of this section provide the setting by describing the tests of ability and attainment taken by these boys and girls, the ages at which they left school and their successes in the General Certificate of Education examinations.

As work in the primary schools is mainly concerned with acquiring basic educational skills, progress can be measured relatively easily. At the secondary stage however pupils acquire knowledge of a more subtle type which is less subject to direct assessment. In this study we are able to gauge a pupil's attainment only by means of standardized tests, General Certificate of Education examination results* and teachers' reports. These assessments are academic, and, as more information becomes available, they will be amplified in future publications to show educational achievement and progress in the wider context of employment and social life.

The tests given to the pupils when they were eight and eleven years old are described in Appendix I of *The Home and the School* (Douglas, 1964). They were group paper and pencil tests individually administered by the teachers or, in a few instances, by educational psychologists. At eight they consisted of tests of picture intelligence, sentence completion, reading and vocabulary. At eleven the reading and vocabulary tests were repeated, the picture intelligence was replaced by an intelligence test, containing both verbal and non-verbal

* We are aware that the standards of Boards and subjects differ, but these examinations nevertheless provided a useful though rough measure of achievement for a certain group of pupils and one that is generally recognized.

[15]

items, and the sentence completion was replaced by an arithmetic test. At fifteen years the four tests used were verbal and non-verbal intelligence, reading and mathematics; a full account of the reliability and validity of the fifteen year tests by D. A. Pidgeon is given in Appendix I.

The National Foundation for Educational Research distributed all the tests to the schools, checked them as they came back and standardized the results for us—that is to say, the results were treated so that the mean score on each test was 50 for the whole Survey population and the standard deviation,* 10 (in each instance after allowing for the original method of choosing the sample. See page 8). Aggregate scores were also calculated for each group of tests by taking the average of the four tests given at each age. The standard deviations of these aggregate scores were below those of the individual scores from which they were derived and moreover varied slightly from year to year. This raised additional problems when test performance at one age was compared with that at another. Owing to this they were re-standardized using as the standardizing population only those pupils who had taken the tests at all three ages. These new aggregate scores all have a mean of 50 and a standard deviation of 9·5.

One of the main conclusions reached during the study of the primary school pupils in England and Wales was that between eight and eleven years the middle classes improved in measured ability and attainment compared with the manual working classes. The difference in the standard deviation or spread of the original aggregate test scores at eight and eleven slightly exaggerated this divergence. When this distortion is removed, the relative improvement of the middle class pupils and the relative deterioration of the manual working class is slightly reduced, though it is still far from negligible; during these three years, the two social classes move apart by 12 per cent of the original difference between them.

The changes in the scores for the different ability and attainment tests are of greater interest than the overall assessment given by a comparison of the aggregate test results. When scores in the picture intelligence test given at eight are compared with those in the non-

* See Glossary. To convert T scores to IQs the following formula may be used: IQ $= 25 + 1·5$ (T score).

[16]

verbal part of the intelligence test given at eleven, the gap between the social classes at eleven is 55 per cent greater than the gap observed three years earlier, whereas in both reading and vocabulary the gap widens by considerably less, approximately 9 per cent. Thus by far the greatest divergence between the social classes is in the non-verbal test results.

When the pupils are grouped into those from middle and those from manual working class families, they are also divided to some extent by their average ability in the tests, those from middle class homes being as a group superior in all tests to the rest. A group of pupils whose scores are above average on one test would be expected for purely statistical reasons to make lower scores when re-tested, and the higher the first score the more the second would be depressed. As a consequence of this regression effect, the average scores of the middle class pupils should be lower on the second testing than on the first, whereas those of the manual working class pupils, whose scores on the first testing are below average, should be higher on the second. This however does not happen; indeed the reverse is true, for the middle class pupils show a relative improvement and the manual working class a relative deterioration between eight and eleven years. The observed changes are contrary to expectation, and if allowances were made for the effects of regression, the divergence of the social classes would be greater than that described. The whole problem of regression is complicated and probably involves regression to the means of the individual groups, as well as to the population mean, and we have not tried to resolve it in this book.

The following social class comparisons of test performance at different ages should be regarded as approximations to the real trends, which they probably underestimate. The divergence in measured ability and attainment between the ages of eight and eleven of the middle and manual class pupils was originally explained in terms of home and school influences; the parents' interest which exerted a substantial effect on test performance at eight exerted an even more pronounced one at eleven. Similarly the academic record of the primary school had an important effect at both ages but more so at eleven. It was recognized however that this environmental explanation might have to be modified when further information

[17]

became available. We are now in a position to re-examine our earlier conclusions in the light of the fifteen year test results.

In the primary schools the main divergence in attainment was between the middle class as a whole and the manual working class as a whole. These two groups of pupils have been further subdivided by the education and social origins of their parents into upper and lower sections.* The upper middle and the lower manual working class families have each retained their characteristics over two generations. They set the extreme middle class and the extreme manual working class patterns, whereas the lower middle class have some manual working class characteristics and the upper manual working class some middle class characteristics.

Diagram I plots the average scores at the ages of eight, eleven and fifteen of pupils in England and Wales grouped by social class. Scores for non-verbal intelligence and reading are given at each of the three ages, scores for vocabulary at the first two ages only, and

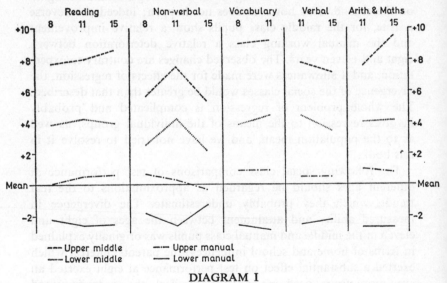

DIAGRAM I
The individual test scores of pupils in England and Wales grouped by their social class. (Differences from the means of all classes.)

* The definition of these four social classes is given in Appendix III.

for verbal intelligence and for arithmetic and mathematics at eleven and fifteen years. As already described, the social classes diverge in performance between eight and eleven years, particularly in non-verbal intelligence. Between eleven and fifteen the divergence continues for reading and mathematics, and in the latter the upper middle class pupils make considerable progress relative to the rest. In contrast, the average non-verbal intelligence scores for the four social classes are nearer to each other at fifteen than they were at eight; the verbal intelligence scores also converge between eleven and fifteen.

That the attainment tests should show a less marked pattern of social change than the non-verbal intelligence tests is unexpected. Some other studies however have reported that intelligence tests are more affected than attainment tests by environmental factors. Wiseman (1964) for example tested a large sample of secondary school pupils and found that when they were grouped by the characteristics of their neighbourhoods, greater environmental differences were recorded in tests of intelligence than of attainment. This, he thought, might arise from the greater drilling in basic subjects such as arithmetic and reading given in areas where educational opportunities are poor—an explanation that is far less likely to hold at the primary school level, where these subjects form the major part of teaching at all types of school and in all areas. Moreover Wiseman sees this situation as arising only when environmental characteristics are assessed from local statistics rather than from the actual homes of the pupils—and it is the homes that were studied in the National Survey.

Different non-verbal tests were used at the three ages, so an explanation of the test score differences might be that the second showed some social bias that was less evident in the first or last. This explanation is however untenable because at Scottish schools (see Diagram II) the non-verbal intelligence test scores of middle and manual working class boys and girls converge between eight and eleven years, as well as between eleven and fifteen years. It is illogical to maintain an explanation based on the social bias of a test in one country when it does not hold in the other.

The most likely explanation of the instability of the non-verbal test results is that they reflect the influence of the secondary selection process itself on the performance of pupils who are about to take the examinations. When pressures to succeed are strong, as in the middle classes, it seems that performance rises. If so, equivalent changes would be expected in other groups of pupils subjected to similar patterns of pressures to do well at the point of selection. When for example those with educationally ambitious parents are

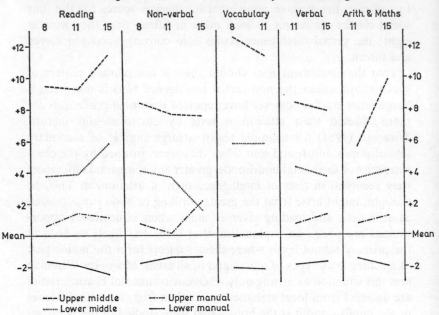

DIAGRAM II

The individual test scores of pupils in Scotland grouped by their social class.
(Differences from the means of all classes.)

contrasted with those whose parents take little interest in their school progress, there is a similar divergence between eight and eleven in non-verbal intelligence, followed by a convergence between eleven and fifteen, whereas in the attainment tests the boys and girls with highly interested parents show a similar relative improvement over the rest throughout their primary and secondary school careers.

On this explanation, when there is no secondary selection in an area there should also be no social class divergence in the non-verbal intelligence test results between eight and eleven years. In Scotland, pupils are selected for their secondary schools a year later than in England and Wales and have moreover a greater chance of starting a 5-year grammar-type course; selection tensions therefore are probably less. On the other hand there is a tradition of teaching the basic subjects from almost the start of school life in Scotland and as the pupils progress through the primary schools there is a gradual release of pressure; in contrast the pressures exerted on pupils in the South tend to increase. The test performance of pupils in the two countries fits this description. In Scotland, the gap between the social classes in non-verbal intelligence is largest at eight and progressively narrows at eleven and fifteen years, whereas in England and Wales, as we have seen, it is widest at eleven and smallest at fifteen. In the attainment tests there is no divergence of the social classes in Scotland between eight and eleven in either reading or vocabulary, but between eleven and fifteen years the middle class pupils move ahead in reading.*

The contrasting performance of pupils in these two countries confirms the view that the changes in non-verbal intelligence test scores of English and Welsh pupils between the ages of eight and eleven are a by-product of secondary selection. They indicate considerable test sophistication among pupils who are anxious to get selective school places. It seems that, when there are incentives to perform well in tests, a non-verbal intelligence test may be a less effective discriminator than an attainment test, at eleven years at any rate.

Social class differences in test performances are at each age less in intelligence than in attainment. This is particularly so at fifteen when the social class gap in attainment is at a maximum and in measured intelligence at a minimum. The difference between the scores made in attainment and in intelligence may be taken as a rough indication of the extent to which pupils in the different social classes are doing better or worse in their school work than would be expected. In this sense, the amount of 'over-' or 'under-achievement' may be assessed. The upper middle class pupils then stand out as showing the best achievement in both reading and mathematics and the lower manual working class as showing the worst. At each

* Horobin, Oldman and Bytheway (1967) report similar findings for Aberdeen children.

age the social class differences are in the same direction, but they are most marked at fifteen when the upper middle class pupils, in particular, are conspicuous for their high achievement.

The extent to which pupils from the four social classes make different use of the available opportunities is discussed in the next chapter when we describe the ages at which they leave school and their successes in the General Certificate of Education.

Chapter Four

School Leaving and G.C.E. Results

Some boys and girls may genuinely need an environment that their schools cannot give, and 'Where school life produces not passing fits of revolt but a real and continuous sense of frustration, the right thing is to leave' (Central Advisory Council for Education, 1954). Those who leave because they are antagonistic to school do not necessarily give up academic work, since they can continue their studies as students in technical colleges and colleges of further education, both of which offer, among other subjects, 'O' and 'A' level courses. These colleges are becoming increasingly popular alternatives to the sixth forms in schools. In 1965—when they were nineteen and a half years old—93 pupils were still at school, and there were also 33 at technical colleges, colleges of further education or with tutors studying for 'O', 'A' and 'S' level examinations.

At some period between the ages of fifteen and sixteen and a half, 3 per cent of both boys and girls entered technical, tutorial, art or secretarial colleges or colleges of further education. Some were studying combined secretarial and academic courses. It was seldom possible to separate those on academic-type courses from the rest and in the following assessments of the loss of potential talent through early or premature leaving all full-time students are included with those still at school. Pupils at special and approved schools are excluded as they normally remain at school after the statutory leaving age.

The boys and girls in the National Survey reached fifteen early in March 1961 and those who left school at the minimum age did so at Easter, one term before the end of the academic year. Approximately half the pupils left school at the earliest opportunity and a further 10 per cent at the end of the summer term. After this there was a year during which relatively few left, followed by a further substantial fall-out at the end of the five year secondary school course at sixteen years four months; 24 per cent of the boys and 23 per cent of the girls were still in full-time education at sixteen and a half years either at school or college. The fall-out during the fifth year included some entering trade apprenticeships that by tradition begin at sixteen and end at twenty-one. Apart from these, the number of mid-fifth-year leavers is small, for most of those still at school or college at the beginning of the year were intending to sit some 'O' level examinations. For convenience we shall use the terms 'completed the session 1961/2' and 'began the session 1962/3'. The first includes all those who would normally have had the opportunity to sit the 'O' level examinations after a five-year secondary school course (or four years in Scotland). The second refers to those who were still at school one term later, in other words, those who stayed on after the normal age of sitting the 'O' level examinations. The majority of these would be entering the sixth form.

The heavy losses through early leaving occur largely in the manual working classes—only 36 per cent of the lower manual working class pupils remained at school after the statutory leaving age. Owing to this differential fall-out there is a rapid change in the social background of those still at school after the age of fifteen. This is shown by the increase in the proportion of upper middle class pupils from 5 per cent of all those at school up to the age of fifteen, to 12 per cent of all those completing the session 1961/2 and to 15 per cent of those starting the session 1962/3.

One reason why the middle class boys and girls stay on longer at school is that they are academically more able, and even when comparisons are made between pupils of similar measured ability and attainment, the social class differences are still marked. This even holds for the pupils of high ability,* and is in contrast with our findings at the point of secondary selection.† At the age of transfer pupils of high ability had an equal chance of reaching grammar schools from whatever social class they came. But there is a heavy

* The term 'pupils of high ability' will always refer to those with aggregate test scores of 60 or more at fifteen years (i.e. the top 16%).
† See Table 4.

[24]

loss even at the highest levels of ability through relatively early leaving from the poorer families. Thus 50 per cent of the lower manual working class pupils of high ability have left school by the end of the session 1961/2, compared with only 10 per cent and 22 per cent respectively of the able upper and lower middle class pupils. From this it is clear that many manual working class pupils, who have the ability to benefit from a sixth year at school or college, are failing to do so.

Social class differences are even greater among those at the border-line level of ability for grammar school entry.* 38 per cent of this group started the session 1962/3 and of these 53 per cent are middle class. Indeed over four-fifths of the upper middle class pupils at this level of ability were still at school at the beginning of the academic year 1962/3, compared with one-fifth of the lower manual working class. Even at the lower ability ranges the majority of upper middle class pupils remain at school after the minimum leaving age; 69 per cent of those whose scores show them to be of average ability or just below stayed at school at least until the end of the session 1961/2 and 42 per cent were still at school one term later—the corresponding percentages for the lower manual working class are 12 per cent and 4 per cent.

The above figures probably understate the loss of academic talent through early leaving for they are based on assessments of ability and attainment made at fifteen, just before the pupils reached the statutory leaving age. The test results at eight or eleven might have given a more realistic picture of the potential ability of these pupils; the figures already given are however striking enough as they stand.

The social class pattern of leaving may be summarized by saying that the upper middle class pupils were two and a half times as likely to stay on after the minimum leaving age as the lower manual working class pupils, four times as likely to complete the session 1961/2 and nearly six times as likely to start session 1962/3. Part of these differences is explained by the higher measured ability of the upper middle class boys and girls, but even when groups of similar ability are compared, the upper middle class pupils were approximately twice as likely to stay on at each age.

* The borderline level includes those pupils with aggregate test scores of 55–59 in the fifteen-year tests.

The results of the G.C.E. 'O' level examinations give a rough measure of academic success for the pupils who stayed on to the end of the session 1961/2, for by this stage the majority of those who are going to take these examinations have already done so. In the independent schools many will have taken the examinations one year earlier than this, though in the secondary modern schools some will take them later. The pupils, on the basis of their General Certificate results, have been divided into three groups; first, those who did not succeed in getting any certificate by the end of the session 1961/2, whether they took the examination or not; second, those who got a 'good' certificate (namely passes in at least four subjects covering three or more of the four main academic fields*—English Language, a Science subject, Mathematics and a foreign language other than Welsh); third, those who had passed in at least one subject but did not gain a good certificate.

1,168 pupils in the educational sample gained one or more passes in the G.C.E. 'O' level examination. In addition 312 were successful in examinations of a lower standard set by other recognized bodies. We shall not be discussing these 312 because of the highly variable standards of the examining bodies and of the differing policies of headmasters in entering candidates. The position would have been different if the new Certificate of Secondary Education had been in existence at the time of this study.

The achievement of pupils of high ability in each of the four social classes is shown in Table 4; 77 per cent of upper middle class pupils get a good certificate, compared with 37 per cent of lower manual working class pupils. The position is slightly less extreme when all certificate holders are considered; 94 per cent of the upper middle class pupils of high ability and 69 per cent of the lower manual working class gained a certificate of some kind.

Differences in measured ability explain only part of the social class differences in 'O' level results. Among the pupils of high ability the proportion of the upper middle class achieving a good certificate is twice that of the lower manual working class, and discrepancies in achievement are even greater at the slightly lower levels of ability. For instance, the upper middle class are three times as likely as the

* Those proceeding direct to the Advanced or Higher level at seventeen years and who were successful were credited with a relevant pass or passes at 'O' level.

[26]

lower manual working class to achieve a good certificate if their ability is at the borderline level for grammar school admission, and thirteen times as likely to achieve a certificate of some sort if they are of just below average ability.*†

When the pupils were fifteen their teachers picked out those who, in their view, had the ability to profit from higher education,‡ the mothers were asked if they wished them to go on to full-time study and the pupils themselves also answered questions about the courses they intended to take after leaving school. Taking only the pupils of high ability 91 per cent of those from the upper middle class were regarded by their teachers as capable of benefiting from higher education, but only 69 per cent of those from the lower manual working class; in both instances almost exactly these proportions later gained one or more passes at 'O' level. It seems that the teachers' views of their pupils, once attainment has been taken into account, correspond closely to their G.C.E. performance. The upper middle class mothers are also in good agreement, both with the teachers and the examination results; 93 per cent of those who have sons or daughters of high ability want them to continue with full-time higher education after leaving school. The lower manual working class mothers of children of high ability however take a less ambitious view; 59 per cent want higher education for their sons and daughters —10 per cent fewer than the teachers. The expressed intentions of the pupils themselves are more modest and probably nearer the real outcome. In each social class fewer pupils wish to continue with full-time education after leaving school than either the teachers recommend or the mothers would wish, the discrepancy being greatest in the lower manual working class.

The social class inequalities in opportunity observed in the primary schools have increased in the secondary and extend, in a way which was not evident at the time of secondary selection, even to the highest levels of ability. It seems that the able boys and girls from manual working class families, although encountering no obstacles at entry to the selective secondary schools, have been

---

* See Table 4.

† I.e. 45–49 aggregate test scores at fifteen years.

‡ At this early age all these assessments of the eventual outcome are unreliable but nevertheless show consistent trends.

[27]

heavily handicapped in their later secondary school careers through relatively early leaving and poor examination results. A substantial proportion of the manual working class pupils get an 'O' level certificate of some sort, but relatively few get a good one. In their aspirations for further education the manual working class pupils also fall considerably short of their teachers' hopes.

This relative lack of educational progress and attainment perhaps stems from low ambitions on the part of the manual working class pupils and their parents. It is a problem that all schools must face and one that will not necessarily diminish as comprehensive schools become widespread. In a selective system the able child from a home which does not value education is supported to some extent by the ethos of the grammar school, and by the attitude of the staff and other pupils—education is valued and homework and study are taken for granted. In future however when all pupils are under the same roof, the able boy or girl who lacks parental support may absorb the values of his neighbourhood and, when these are easy going, may wish to start work at the same age as his local friends, and so not try to do well.

Chapter Five

Boys and Girls

In the primary schools boys and girls are for the most part taught together in the same class-rooms, and their measured ability and attainments are similar. The girls, on the average, make rather higher scores than the boys in all tests, except for vocabulary at eight and eleven years. Their advantage was however slightly less at the older age. The primary school teachers assessed the girls as having a more serious attitude to their work and as being more satisfactory pupils than the boys, who were more often reported as restless and inattentive in class. The teachers also thought that a larger proportion of the girls than of the boys would benefit from grammar school education; indeed they would have sent nearly a third more girls than boys to grammar school. The actual distribution of places of course did not follow this pattern. Slightly more girls than boys were given grammar school places, but this was offset by a greater proportion of boys at technical schools.*

Some parents, who had been content to allow their daughters to go to maintained primary schools, sent them to independent schools later when they failed to get a grammar school place. Accordingly when independent schools are included with grammar, direct grant and technical schools, there are rather more girls than boys receiving selective education; this holds in each social class.

Other studies have shown that up to the age of eleven girls reach a higher standard than boys in tests of the basic school subjects, whereas at later ages boys make higher scores on the average than girls in non-verbal tests, and reach a higher level of attainment in arithmetic and mathematics. These differences between the ability

* See Table 2.

[29]

and attainment of boys and girls at secondary school are confirmed in the present study. At the age of fifteen the boys make higher scores than the girls in non-verbal intelligence and mathematics, and are ahead even in reading which is traditionally thought to be a girl's rather than a boy's subject. It is only in verbal intelligence that the girls have the higher scores.* These differences hold to approximately the same extent in each social class.

The ages at which boys and girls leave school, up to the age of sixteen and a half at any rate, do not reflect these sex differences. This may be owing to the secretarial and art courses provided for girls in many secondary schools and, also, perhaps to the inclusion among those 'still at school' of pupils who left school to take these courses in other institutions. Rather more girls than boys leave as soon as they are fifteen, but this is balanced by a heavier loss of boys one term later at the end of the summer session.† The girls of high ability were just as likely as the boys of high ability to start the session 1962/3, and at the lower ranges of ability were more likely to do so. Among the less able pupils it was particularly girls from the upper middle class families who stayed on; 70 per cent of those who scored less than 55 in the tests started the session 1962/3, as compared with only 47 per cent of upper middle class boys of comparable ability.

In assessing the likely performance in the General Certificate of Education 'O' level examinations the teachers expected more girls than boys to pass in at least one 'O' level subject, though they forecast that the average standard reached by the boys would be higher. These fifteen year predictions were not quite borne out by the actual results. When all boys are compared with all girls, more of the former get a good certificate, but the proportions gaining a certificate, regardless of the number of passes, are roughly equal. This is the position in the maintained schools but in the independent schools the girls achieve less than the boys at every level of measured ability (see Chapter VIII). The fact that fewer girls get good certificates is largely explained by their lower pass rates in mathematics and science subjects. It may be objected that our definition of a good certificate unfairly discriminates against the girls because it requires a pass in

* See Table 5.
† See Table 2.

[30]

either mathematics or a science, which some regard as boys' rather than girls' subjects. At the age of sixteen however it is not unreasonable to expect that girls as well as boys should understand the basic principles of one, if not both, of these subjects. Indeed the able girls, though it should be remembered that there are fewer of them, are slightly more likely than the able boys to gain a good certificate.* At lower levels of ability the girls, although they get no more good certificates than the boys, are less likely to fail completely and this is particularly so in the middle classes, where it seems that an 'O' level pass has more vocational value for a girl than a boy.

Girls reach physical maturity earlier than boys, and this has been seen by many as a reason for the flagging performance of the former in the later years at school. Early maturing pupils however whether boys or girls, make higher scores in the tests than late maturing ones, get more and better 'O' level certificates and stay on longer at school. Accordingly, early physical maturity can hardly be used to explain the differences between the educational performance of boys and girls (see Chapter XIX).

Between eleven and fifteen the boys become increasingly aware that what they learn at school will influence their future careers, the sort of employment for which they will be suited and the level of training that will be open to them on leaving school. In contrast, the girls see themselves as entering work that requires relatively little specialized training and will last for only a few years before marriage. The different job prospects of boys and girls are reflected in the varying school curricula available to them. For example where many of the pupils leave to take up secretarial and clerical work, the girls' schools often run general sixth form courses. It is to be expected, then, that boys and girls have rather different views on entering full-time higher education. This is indeed so; of those of high ability at the age of fifteen, 62 per cent of the boys and 54 per cent of the girls said that they wished to continue full-time education after leaving school. This difference in the aspirations of boys and girls is also evident in the views of both the mothers and the teachers.

In 1965, during visits to some of these young people at the universities, we had the opportunity to discuss the reasons why the girls' performance falls off at secondary school. The comments of some of

* See Table 6.

[31]

these highly intelligent students are revealing. There are two main areas of criticism—the poor teaching in girls' schools and the waning interest of girls who increasingly see their adult roles as being played in the home rather than at work.

In the following comments, which are fairly typical of the majority made by university students, girls who have just left the sixth form and been among the most successful pupils are critical of their former mistresses.

'The trouble with girls' schools is that the unmarried teacher comes in just before she gets married and then goes away and has a baby and so we have a continual break and change in our school careers. Also these young teachers are more interested in their families than in their careers.'

'I found the young staff more stimulating, but they were usually just drifting through. They used illustrations from real life and told you funny stories connected with the subject, whereas the old mistresses just read the book.'

'The indifference is a vicious circle—the girls are indifferent because the lessons are boring, unrelated to anything, and the teachers find that pupils are indifferent and therefore become boring. Not so in a boys' school.'

'At fifteen all that kept me at school was my parents. I had not lost interest in the subject, just in the way it was being taught in school.'

That it was not only the teaching in girls' schools that was at fault is suggested by the following comments, from both girls and boys. They illustrate the tailing-off of interest in the more senior forms.

'There's the feeling between the second and fifth form that if you work you are a swot, and this is stronger for girls because the majority of them aren't going to stay on after the fifth and the small minority who are, are therefore subjected to this majority.'

'Girls were quite content to tail-off into a not-so-interesting job or training college or something like that, when they could sometimes get much further.'

'I think girls realize about thirteen that even though it's equal opportunity, they are expected to marry and bring up children. This feeling is still very strong.'

'The majority of girls only want a certain amount of education

[32]

and then want to get married, and so there isn't a great deal of bother taken over the other ones who really want to get on.'

It is generally recognized that during their later years at school many girls lose interest in their work and the beginnings of this are reflected in the lower test scores recorded for them at fifteen in the present study. The full effects of this decline in interest will however be more clearly seen in the proportions taking 'A' levels and entering higher education.

There was general agreement among the boys and girls we talked to that many girls learn by memorizing material whether they understand it or not, whereas boys are more likely to try to master the underlying principles.

As one girl said:

'We work like mad; we learn things off parrot fashion; I find the tension in examinations is such that I have to learn it off parrot fashion in order to be able to write it down; I never knew that boys did not do this too.'

A boy said:

'You cannot help but be impressed by women, they work very hard, but in tutorials a lot of them are incapable of applying what they have learnt if you ask them questions.'

Another boy said:

'I think a woman is far more concerned with learning material and getting it up for the examination than assimilating it.'

Perhaps this is more a reflection of the type of girl who gets to the university, than of the intellectual approach of women as a whole.

The raising of academic targets for the girls requires a re-modelling of parental attitudes, a new approach in the schools and higher though realistic aspirations among the pupils. Solution for this problem partly lies in teaching—in the co-educational schools for example (see page 71) the attainments of girls up to sixteen and a half are, except in mathematics, as good as the boys'. It also lies partly in changing girls' perceptions of their ability in certain subjects. Although the girls, on the average, are below the boys in mathematics, a few find this is their best subject. Out of 32 university mathematics students there are 13 women; this is rather more than would be expected from the ratio of all men to all women undergraduates and suggests that, given the right type of teaching—which might be different from that given to boys—the girls could become as interested in mathematics and achieve as much as the boys. There is however a danger that the academic progress of girls in the future may fall further behind the boys. The pattern of early marriage is likely to continue, and the increasing importance given to mathematics and technical subjects may also discourage girls from competing in fields that appear to be inappropriate.

Perhaps the main problem is the attitude of the parents; this is well illustrated in the independent schools (see Chapter VIII). When parents send their sons to fee-paying schools their main aim is that they should receive first-rate teaching, which will fully develop their potentialities and open the way to interesting and worth-while training and employment. The public schools certainly meet these requirements; they take some boys whose measured ability is below that required for grammar school and give them an excellent academic education. The same types of parent however seem to seek other advantages when they send their daughters to fee-paying schools, advantages that are more social than academic. Even in the independent girls' schools which belong to the Headmistresses' Association, the average progress is disappointing and academic success is lower than in the girls' grammar schools. The conclusion is that middle class parents put a higher value on the education of their sons than their daughters.

Chapter Six

The Progress and Attainment
of Pupils at Selective Schools

The majority of the pupils in this study received their secondary education in a system which allocated 24 per cent to grammar, direct grant or technical schools and 58 per cent to secondary modern. In addition, 11 per cent went to comprehensive or bilateral, 5 per cent to independent and 2 per cent to approved or special schools.* This chapter is concerned with the 29 per cent who were at grammar, direct grant, technical or independent schools at the age of fifteen years. All these schools select their pupils to a greater or lesser extent by ability and, in the case of the independent schools, by their parents' income and aspirations as well. All place a strong emphasis on academic subjects.

That the selective and secondary modern schools should be discussed in separate chapters with no direct comparisons between them may seem regrettable, but it inevitably follows from the selection process itself. At the primary schools, children study mainly the basic subjects of reading, writing and arithmetic, and their progress at this stage can to some extent be adequately assessed by means of standardized tests of attainment; in the secondary schools however there is no similar uniformity. When pupils are transferred to their respective selective or non-selective schools they meet a whole variety of courses which offer widely different curricula, opportunities and stimulation. The variation in educational possibilities, even between different selective schools or between different secondary moderns, is great, while between these two major types of school it is so wide as to make comparisons almost meaningless.

* See Table 2. These figures refer to the complete sample and are population estimates.

[35]

Problems are raised by the fact that pupils are selected for different types of secondary school by measured ability, examinations and teachers' reports. When for example grammar and secondary modern pupils, who were of comparable measured ability in our tests at eleven and in the borderline group for admission to grammar school, are re-tested at fifteen, the former have improved their performance in each test and the latter have fallen behind, which gives a clear impression of better academic progress in the selective schools. This however is not necessarily the correct interpretation of these test score changes. There is no reason to believe that the same pupils who improved their performance at grammar school would have deteriorated if they had been at secondary modern, or that the modern school pupils would have improved if they had been at grammar. The ambiguity arises from the fact that, though this borderline group made similar scores in the National Survey tests, the two groups of pupils were also sorted out by the official selection procedure in such a way, that those who maintained their high level of performance in these additional tests and examinations were allocated to grammar schools, whereas those who were more variable in their performance went to secondary modern. The former on their past record would be expected to maintain or improve their position during the next four years, while the latter, whose ability may have been over-estimated by our eleven year tests, would be expected to lose ground.

Grammar and secondary modern school pupils could be validly compared if only those at the borderline level of ability for admission to grammar school were allotted at random to the two types of school; and this does not, and obviously cannot, happen. At each level of ability the teachers' reports, parents' wishes and local availability of places will influence the outcome. It would indeed be surprising if most of the grammar school pupils did not benefit from the smaller classes, the stress on academic subjects and the intellectual stimulation of their class-mates: perhaps this is why they draw ahead in reading and mathematics rather than in measured intelligence. For the less able pupils at grammar schools these benefits may be illusory, indeed it can be argued that pupils at the top of a secondary modern school have an advantage over those at the bottom of a grammar. There is no direct supporting evidence for this from the National Survey data, though it is noteworthy that many of the pupils who transferred late from secondary modern to grammar schools did well. These are however predominantly from middle class families, hard working and with highly interested parents.

Within the selective schools there are wide variations in staffing, amenities, buildings and academic record which are in turn associated with the ability of the pupils enrolled and the social backgrounds from which they come. After a detailed examination of the relation between the school characteristics and test performance, it appeared that the most useful way to classify the schools was into the following three groups.

(a) Those with less than 70 per cent graduate members on the teaching staff;

(b) Those with 70 to 79 per cent;

(c) Those with 80 per cent or more.

These three groups also differ in the number of teaching vacancies reported and the standard of equipment and buildings; on the whole the schools with the highest proportion of graduate teachers are the best staffed and equipped and those with the smallest proportion are the worst.

The three groups of schools also attract different types of pupils. The schools with the highest proportion of graduates have the highest proportion of middle class pupils; the girls however are less likely to be taught by graduates than the boys. Even after allowances are made for these social class and sex differences,† the average ability on entry shows wide differences between the three types of school.* Those at schools with a high proportion of graduate teachers make, on the whole, higher scores in all the tests than those at schools with a low proportion. These differences are not the same for all the tests. In intelligence and reading, they are large, but in arithmetic it is only the pupils going to schools that have less than 70 per cent graduate teachers who fall below the others. During the succeeding four years the differences in the average performance of pupils at these three groups of schools narrow. In the intelligence test there is a general deterioration between eleven and fifteen, which

* See Table 7.

† See Appendix II of *The Home and the School.*

[37]

can probably be explained by the artificially high scores made by the educationally ambitious pupils in the non-verbal tests given at eleven. In contrast, the scores made in the attainment tests as a whole improve, probably reflecting the results of the academic orientation of the selective schools.

It seems then that in the limited context of these tests there is little change, between eleven and fifteen years, in the relative positions of the average scores of pupils at the three groups of selective schools, once their initial selection has been taken into account. Mathematics and reading however are only a small sample of the skills acquired by a successful selective secondary school pupil, and a better indication of the relative success of these schools is given by the 'O' level results and leaving patterns.

The proportion of graduates on the staff of selective schools is at first sight associated with G.C.E. 'O' level results and leaving age. These differences are however largely illusory for they depend for the most part on the differential recruitment of pupils to the three types of school. The schools with the highest proportion of graduates on their staff attract more of their pupils from the middle classes and also a greater number of the more able: once these two factors are allowed for, differences between the attainment and progress of pupils in the three types of school are greatly reduced. They are however still considerable for the boys, though for the girls it is only the total 'O' level results that differentiate between pupils at the three types of school. It may well be that in their sixth form courses the advantages of being at schools with a high proportion of graduate teachers will be even more evident.

The report *Early Leaving*, published in 1954 by the Central Advisory Council for Education, described a group of pupils who entered grammar and direct grant schools in 1946. The outstanding finding of this study was the profound influence of the home on the school careers of the pupils. The social class differences found in the attainment of boys and girls in grammar schools were only partly explained by the higher ability of middle class pupils at entry. Throughout the time at grammar school, there was a change in attainment, which resulted in a clustering of middle class pupils towards the upper end of each year group and of manual working

[38]

class pupils towards the lower. It seemed that the working class boys and girls who had reached the grammar schools, often against the pressures of their homes and friends, were severely handicapped in their later academic progress. In the remainder of this chapter, we show the extent to which family background and school progress are associated in the present group of pupils, who entered their selective schools 11 years later than those described in *Early Leaving*.

The mean test scores of the pupils in each social class have been adjusted for the effects of the varying proportion of graduate staff and the sex of the pupils. In this way we are able to compare the progress of selective school pupils from each type of family background unaffected by the quality of the schools they attended. When they enter the selective schools, the average adjusted intelligence and reading scores of pupils from the four social classes differ considerably, the upper middle class having the highest average scores and the manual working class the lowest. In arithmetic however the scores of the eleven year old manual working class pupils, when they enter the selective secondary schools, are as good as those of the middle class, so that in relation to their intelligence test results the former are over-achievers in this subject.*

During the succeeding four years the social classes grow further apart in both the attainment tests. The upper middle class pupils have, by fifteen, a considerable advantage over the rest in mathematics, whereas the manual working class pupils, who started off at eleven with high arithmetic scores, have deteriorated in relation to the pupils from the three other social classes. In the reading test, the advantage which the upper middle class pupils have on entry is considerably increased during the subsequent four years, whereas the lower middle, and upper and lower manual working class pupils retain their positions relative to each other.

All the fifteen year old pupils at selective schools do better in the attainment tests than would be expected from their scores in the non-verbal, or intelligence, test. There is however a steady social class gradient in the extent of high achievement. For example the upper middle class pupils on the average score nearly two and a half points more in mathematics than in intelligence, whereas the lower manual working class pupils score only half a point more.

* See Table 8.

[39]

For the reading test, the relative figures are two points more for the upper middle class and just over one-third of a point more for the lower manual working class, while the lower middle and the upper manual working class pupils lie in between. In other words, the achievement of pupils at selective schools, defined as the difference between non-verbal intelligence and attainment in reading and mathematics, is greatly influenced by the type of family from which they come.*

The differences between the social classes in the ability and attainment tests at eleven and fifteen years are similar whatever the type of school, and there is no suggestion that the manual working class pupils are at less of a disadvantage in schools with a high proportion of graduate teachers.

In contrast to the test scores, the leaving and 'O' level results show that although the lower manual working class pupils get relatively poor results and are the early leavers in each type of school, they are less handicapped in the schools with the highest proportion of graduates on the teaching staff. For example 56 per cent of the lower manual working class boys and girls at selective schools with few graduate teachers were expected by their ability to achieve a general certificate of some sort, whereas only 37 per cent did so—a difference of 19 per cent. In the schools with most graduates, on the other hand, 81 per cent were expected by their ability to achieve some certificate and in fact 78 per cent did so.† Even larger differences are found if, instead of all certificate holders, only those with good certificates are considered. The inference from this is not necessarily that the lower manual working class boys and girls have benefited preferentially from better standards of teaching; perhaps they were more rigorously selected in the first place. In *The Home and the School* it was shown that when competition was keen and grammar school places were in short supply, the manual working class pupils were at a particular disadvantage, for the successful candidates will have been chosen partly for personality traits and family circumstances that in the view of the selectors are good predictors of later academic success.

In the present study, the change in the ability and attainment of

* See Table 9.
† See Table 10.

[40]

pupils in the four social classes and the differences in patterns of leaving are similar to those described 11 years before in the *Early Leaving* Report. They are of approximately the same size in spite of the fact that immediately after the end of the war, when the Early Leaving sample were entering their grammar and direct grant schools, the rate of internal migration was high and this might have been expected to upset the smooth course of secondary education.

We were able to make a special study of early leavers from grammar school a year or so after these young men and women had entered employment. Their academic record in the secondary schools before their premature departure, was uniformly unsuccessful. Their test scores showed general deterioration between eleven and fifteen years, their attendance was poor and they were also likely to be reported by those who taught them as less punctual, obedient and amenable to discipline (especially the girls), more restless and more likely to day-dream than the other pupils.

We contacted both the early leavers themselves and the heads of their schools. None of the boys and girls mentioned lack of ability as a cause of leaving or thought that their school work had been too difficult for them. The majority said they could have managed it and most felt on looking back that it would have been better for them if they had continued their education for a year or so. 'I have regretted leaving school before taking the G.C.E., I now go to evening classes but feel I have missed something in the social way by leaving school before my time.' A few thought they would have had difficulty in finishing their academic course. Their most common reason for leaving was the desire to start a career, with lack of interest in school work and dislike of school coming second. This is typified by one youngster who wrote: 'I thought work would be more interesting.'

Some insight into the reasons for their lack of interest in school is given by their answers to what they liked and disliked most about school. The likes for both boys and girls were limited to a few fields: of the boys who mentioned some things about school which they liked, more than half gave sport as their favourite activity, while the dislikes were centred mainly on homework and discipline. The girls appeared to have found more both to like and to dislike about their schools, but it is the dislikes that come through with force and strength of feeling: 'You're just one on the class list to be got through

[41]

the G.C.E.!' 'I disliked the unnecessary discipline, such as fifteen year old girls having to sit crosslegged on floors. They feel very uncomfortable.' 'I left school when I did because I just couldn't stand the teachers and their attitude towards the pupils.' 'I disliked most being treated rather like a twelve year old.'

The heads refer more often to lack of parental interest and poor family circumstances than to lack of academic ability: 'Perhaps the illness of her father, since dead, had some bearing on her anxiety to become a wage earner.' 'Her parents could have had little conception of what it all meant.' In writing about girls, almost all the heads mentioned lack of enthusiasm and interest, and nearly half of them said that the girls had left because they wished to start work. This is illustrated by the following comments: 'We found in school that she had the ability to continue but had little interest and was determined to leave.' 'She was well supplied with ability but her interests lay elsewhere. My impression was that the trivia of feminine life had a strong pull for her, and that her undoubted ability in art contributed towards a greater concern for clothing, etc., than for anything we could offer.' Dislike of school and a rebellious nature was also attributed by the heads to half the boys and a fifth of the girls.

A good school should compensate in some respects for a poor home, but when the school is disliked by the pupils obviously little can be done to encourage them to stay on. Perhaps the fact that some of the boys and girls see in retrospect that a longer school life would have been beneficial to them may mean that when their own children have to make the choice, they will encourage them to stay on and take the chance that they themselves had missed.

Chapter Seven

The Progress and Attainment of Pupils at Secondary Modern Schools

The secondary modern schools which 58 per cent of the boys and girls in the study attended were by no means uniform. They offered their pupils variable opportunities and courses. Their size, buildings and teaching staff all varied greatly as also did the home backgrounds of the pupils on their rolls. Some schools were successful in retaining a substantial proportion of their pupils after the minimum school leaving age and in providing them with the chance to sit the General Certificate of Education examinations, whereas others failed to retain more than a small proportion and had little to offer at a more advanced level to those who did stay on. This variation in opportunity leads to further selection within an apparently unselective group of schools. The middle class parents are less anchored to one locality than the manual working class and it is they who have the determination to choose for their sons and daughters, if they do not get to a selective school, the type of secondary modern which offers the best prospects. As a result there is a high proportion of middle class pupils in the better staffed and better housed secondary modern schools, whereas the pupils from the manual working class, the lower section in particular, are more often found in the secondary modern schools that have poor buildings, workshops and art rooms, and where staff shortages are frequently reported.

Very few pupils (only 2 per cent in this study) are transferred from secondary modern to grammar schools and these come predominantly from middle class homes; in addition, 3 per cent transferred to technical schools and 2 per cent (the majority girls) to independent.

As few upper middle class pupils go to secondary modern schools

[43]

of any type, we have in this chapter combined the two middle classes while retaining the two divisions of the manual working class.

G.C.E. attainment and leaving age are closely related to many of the characteristics of the secondary modern schools. The schools which are most successful within the limits of our criteria are large schools in urban areas with good buildings, art rooms and workshops, medium sized classes and a relatively high proportion of graduates on the staff. More important than all these however is the proportion of pupils who in past years have stayed on after the age of fifteen and it is on this factor that we have grouped the schools into the following categories.

(a) Those which retained less than 10 per cent (poor past record);

(b) Those which retained 10 per cent to 19 per cent (fair past record);

(c) Those which retained 20 per cent or more of their pupils (good past record).

Many of the other characteristics of the schools mentioned above are inherent in this classification—those with a good past record are more frequently boys' schools, have better buildings, more graduate staff and a higher proportion of middle class pupils. In the following comparison of the test performances of pupils at these three types of modern school, allowances are made for the sex of the pupils as well as for their social class.

On entry at eleven there is a statistically significant difference in the average intelligence scores of pupils entering the three types of school. Those entering schools with a good past record were, on the average, of superior intelligence to those at the other two groups of schools, though their performance in the arithmetic and reading tests was not significantly different. Four years later the differences in measured intelligence are much reduced, but the pupils in the schools with a good past record make significantly higher scores in reading and also have an advantage in mathematics, though this does not quite reach significance.*

The secondary modern school pupils in each of these groups of schools make lower scores in both the arithmetic and mathematics tests than in intelligence or reading, and they can be regarded, on

* See Table 11.

[44]

the average, as poor achievers in this subject. Perhaps the special emphasis that seems to have been placed on arithmetic ability when selecting for the grammar schools has led to a dearth of numerate pupils in the secondary modern schools.

While achievement in mathematics was relatively low among pupils in each of the three groups of secondary modern schools, the discrepancy between measured intelligence and mathematics is greatest among those at schools with the worst leaving record and smallest for those at the schools with the best. The reading attainment of pupils at the schools with a poor past record is also below that expected from their intelligence test results, while that of pupils at the other two groups of schools is above. Thus in both mathematics and reading the pupils at the schools with the most favourable pattern of leaving are the best achievers. Taking account however of the wide differences between the facilities and staff provided in these three groups of schools, it is perhaps surprising that the differences in achievement are not greater.*

Wiseman (1964, p. 157) has suggested that the less satisfactory schools drill their pupils in mechanical arithmetic and reading as part of the response to poor staffing, large classes and other inadequacies and difficulties. Moreover since the duller pupils, if they are to be employed, must be literate, every effort will be made to make them so. 'Because the intelligence test is relatively free from the effects of schooling this (the drilling) has little effect on the distribution of I.Q., but raises the average scores on reading and arithmetic in schools in the worst areas. When we now make a survey of the area, we find an "intelligence gradient" corresponding to the "social gradient" as we move from the favoured outer fringe to the deprived centre area. The gradient for attainment however is *less* steep, because of the radical differences in time-table and curriculum between "white" and "black" schools. By the efforts of the teachers, not only has the environmental differential between intelligence and attainment levels been obliterated, but it has actually been reversed.' This as we have seen does not hold in the present study.

There are considerable differences in both age of leaving and general certificate 'O' level results of the boys and girls at the three types of school (those with poor, fair and good past records of

* See Table 12.

[45]

retaining their pupils after fifteen years). The pupils at the group of schools with a good past record were nearly $2\frac{1}{2}$ times as likely to stay after the minimum leaving age as those at schools where the record had been poor and nearly $3\frac{1}{2}$ times as likely to stay to the end of the 1961/2 session. For the G.C.E. examination results the differences are proportionately larger still. Those at schools with a good record were more than 8 times as likely to get a certificate. Some of the superior performances of pupils at the schools with a good record is to be explained by their higher ability, superior family circumstances and the excess of boys: but even so these three factors account for a small part only of these advantages. If selection of pupils were the only source of superior performance in the good schools, which otherwise offered educational opportunities similar to those offered by schools with a poor past record, then the ratios expected would be reduced to less than $1\frac{1}{2}$ times both for staying after the minimum leaving age and for completing the session 1961/2, and $1\frac{1}{2}$ times for gaining at least one 'O' level pass. These expected advantages are much smaller than those quoted above. The influence of the secondary modern schools on these pupils appears to be greatest in the highest forms. This might have been anticipated, for schools that lose most of their pupils at fifteen years are unlikely to be able to make as adequate and satisfactory arrangements for the education of those who do stay on.

The General Certificate of Education does not provide a satisfactory criterion for the achievement of the secondary modern school pupils—indeed it was never meant to. It is interesting nevertheless to note that 6 per cent were successful in one or more subjects but these were by no means all academic subjects—woodwork, needlework, art and other craft subjects are included. With the introduction of the Certificate of Secondary Education, a more varied group of pupils will be officially examined; this will provide assessments of academic ability and attainment for at least another 20 per cent of pupils and will make comparisons easier for research in the future.

By sending their children to the best equipped and best staffed secondary modern schools, the middle classes make fuller use than the manual working classes of the opportunities provided. The next

[46]

question to consider is whether, *within* each of the three groups of secondary modern schools, the middle class pupils are making fuller use of the existing facilities than the manual working class.

When they enter the secondary modern schools the middle class boys and girls make higher scores in the tests of intelligence, arithmetic and reading than the upper or lower manual working class pupils, even after adjustments have been made for type of school and sex. At eleven the middle class pupils at secondary modern schools are however exceptional in having scores for reading and arithmetic that are lower than their intelligence test scores—this is in contrast to the middle class pupils as a whole, who consistently make higher scores in the attainment than in the non-verbal and verbal intelligence tests. It seems therefore that the group of middle class boys and girls entering secondary modern schools includes a high proportion who have done poorly in their school work at the primary stage. The upper manual working class pupils on entry have attainment scores which are rather above their ability scores, while the lower manual working class pupils have attainment scores that are below.*

There are highly significant differences in test performance between the social classes at both eleven and fifteen. At eleven the differences are approximately the same for intelligence, arithmetic and reading, there being just over 3 points of test score between the middle class as a whole and the lower working manual class. At fifteen the intelligence and mathematics scores show similar 3 point differences between the social classes, whereas the reading score difference has increased to nearly 4 points. At this stage the middle class pupils, as well as the upper manual working class, make higher scores in reading than would be expected from their scores in intelligence, but the lower manual working class pupils still read less well than would be expected. In mathematics the average score of the fifteen year old middle class pupils is below their average intelligence score.

The middle class pupils at secondary modern schools stay on longer than the manual working class pupils and are more likely to achieve at least one pass in the General Certificate of Education. 64 per cent of middle class pupils stayed after the minimum leaving

* See Table 13.

[47]

age and 32 per cent stayed at least to the end of the 1961/2 session; this compares with 23 per cent staying after the minimum leaving age and 11 per cent to the end of the 1961/2 session in the lower manual working class. Similarly 13 per cent of the middle class pupils but only 3 per cent of the lower manual working class gained one or more 'O' level pass. These differences are partly explained by the higher measured ability of the middle class pupils and the fact that a greater proportion go to secondary modern schools with academic courses. However when both ability and type of school are allowed for, there are still considerable differences between the achievement of pupils in the social classes. They may be summarized as follows: 3 times as many middle as lower manual working class pupils stayed on at school till the end of the 1961/2 session, whereas on their measured ability and the quality of school they attend only 1½ times as many would be expected to do so. Similarly 4 times as many middle class pupils get an 'O' level certificate, whereas only twice as many would be expected to achieve this. On each criterion then, the fact of being middle class roughly doubles the chances of educational success, even after allowing for differences in measured ability and for the influence of the different types of school.

An important question arises here: are the manual working class pupils less handicapped at some types of school? In other words is there any evidence that good teaching and mixing with pupils who are likely to stay past the minimum leaving age, has a beneficial effect on the boy or girl from a home where education is little valued? Table 14 shows that although the lower manual working class pupils are at a disadvantage relative to the middle class in all types of school, those at schools with a good record are far less handicapped.

Thus the secondary modern schools can do something to make up for the deficiencies of the homes, even more so perhaps than the selective schools, though here again problems of selection are relevant (see page 40). *The Home and the School* showed that good teaching compensates in part for lack of parental interest in the earlier years—and this appears to be also true at the secondary stage.

Chapter Eight
Independent Schools and their Pupils

The independent and private schools in England and Wales play an important part in secondary education, particularly at the older ages and at the level of preparing for university entrance. In Scotland, which has few independent schools of high standing, their contribution to the total effort of secondary education is much smaller and there is in general less social segregation of pupils than south of the border. Many independent schools have a high reputation and are often able to offer higher salaries, hence it is generally thought they are in a position to provide better standards of teaching than those available in the majority of the maintained schools.

It was largely from the public schools themselves that the initiative came for the setting up of the Fleming Committee, who reported in 1944 on the means of developing and extending the association between the public schools and the general educational system. They suggested that these schools should offer a minimum of one-quarter of their yearly intake to boys who had spent two years or more at maintained primary schools; this would be the first step towards making these schools equally accessible to all pupils. On the whole however apart from a few isolated instances the response to this report has been disappointing. Individual schools have made efforts to recruit pupils through the local education authorities, but generally speaking the support they have received has been discouraging. In 1966, another committee with Sir John Newsom at its head was appointed to look into the future of the independent schools and their integration within the maintained school system.

The concern of the Headmasters' Conference for the future of their schools has also been evident in a survey sponsored by them two years before the setting up of the Newsom Committee, with the object of establishing some facts. We will refer to the report of this survey, called *The Public Schools; A Factual Survey* by Graham Kalton (1966), later in this chapter.

Few would dispute that some of the public schools in this country provide an education and training for their pupils that in many respects is second to none: some schools indeed have an international reputation for high standards of education, and these schools also have always been proud of what may loosely be termed their 'training for leadership'. In fact, it is just because of the excellence of some of these schools that their future is in question for, in the climate of today, it seems wrong to many that a small section of the population should be able to buy for their children an education which is unobtainable for the majority. Yet to abolish or distort a system which is acknowledged to be good seems wasteful.

Four per cent of the boys and 6 per cent of the girls in the National Survey were at independent or private as opposed to maintained schools.* This represents a substantial contribution to the total educational facilities available in this country, especially when it is remembered that pupils from the big public schools gain a disproportionately large number of scholarships, exhibitions and places particularly at the older universities.

The wide variety of independent and private schools attended by the Survey members is reflected in the big differences that are found in the proportion of graduate staff and in form size. As a group, the independent schools are smaller than the grammar and so also are the classes, whereas the proportion of graduates on the teaching staff is on the whole considerably lower than in the grammar schools, particularly for the girls. The heads of the independent schools however do not see the low proportion of graduate teachers as reflecting staff shortages; these are more frequently reported from the grammar schools. In particular, the independent girls' schools appear to be more able to get mathematics staff than the girls' grammar schools. The independent boys' schools appear to be better provided than the grammar schools with laboratory, workshop and art room facilities, but, although there are many well equipped independent schools, some have poor amenities and facilities.

* These figures are population estimates for the complete sample.

[50]

Although the G.C.E. results and leaving dates are known for 99 per cent of those at the independent schools, only 63 per cent were tested at fifteen years. In order to provide reasonable numbers for the comparisons that follow, the earlier test information at eight and eleven years has been used to estimate the missing fifteen year scores. In this way, 86 per cent of those at independent schools can be grouped into broad fifteen year old ability bands, either actual or estimated* and their G.C.E. results and leaving dates compared with those for pupils of roughly similar ability at other types of school.

As the independent schools, taken as a whole, recruit their pupils from a wider range of ability than the maintained grammar schools (19 per cent of those at independent schools had at eleven years been allocated to secondary modern schools), it is not unexpected to find that the total 'O' level performance of their pupils is lower than for those at grammar schools. What is unexpected however is that this difference with one exception holds at each level of ability—the boys of high ability at independent schools run contrary to the general pattern for they are slightly more likely than the boys of high ability at grammar schools to get good general certificates—if all certificate holders are taken however those at grammar schools once again as a group are superior.

The discrepancies between the attainment of those in independent and grammar schools are larger for the girls than for the boys; the girls as a whole do not do well academically in independent schools and the level achieved there even by the able girls is disappointing— 46 per cent of those of high ability get a good certificate, compared with 67 per cent of the girls of high ability at grammar schools, and only 74 per cent achieve a certificate of some kind by sixteen and a half years, compared with over 92 per cent.

The proportion of boys starting the session 1962/3 is slightly higher in the independent than in the grammar schools, the main

---

* The boys and girls who failed to complete all the tests tended on the whole to be those of less than average ability; for the independent school pupils however this is not so. Those who completed the fifteen year tests but missed some earlier information were, on the average, of exactly the same ability as those who had completed all tests, and the estimated scores for those who did not sit the fifteen year tests are only slightly below the average scores for the rest of the independent school pupils, and not significantly so.

difference being found in the group of borderline ability for admission to grammar school. In this group, 79 per cent of those at independent schools but only 58 per cent of those at grammar schools start the 1962/3 session. With the girls, those at grammar schools stay on longer.

To contrast the academic performance of independent and private school pupils with those at grammar schools may be thought unsound since one in five of the former was allocated in the 11+ examinations to a secondary modern school, and so cannot be expected to do as well academically as if they had been picked by ability for grammar schools.

It might be better therefore to compare at each level of ability the middle class pupils at independent and private schools (84 per cent of the total) with the middle class pupils at all types of maintained school. It is then found that, at each level of ability, the differences in 'O' level performance between the boys at these two groups of schools are small, with one exception. The boys of high ability at independent schools gain more good certificates than the middle class boys of high ability at all other types of school, though these differences disappear when all certificate holders, and not merely the good ones, are considered. The length of school life for middle class boys at the independent schools is at each level of ability longer than for those at maintained schools.

For the girls a similar comparison yields very different results. The middle class girl of high ability at the maintained school is more, not less likely to get a certificate, this certificate is more likely to be a good one and her school career will also be longer. At lower levels of ability however differences are inconsistent.

The fact that all independent and private schools are grouped together prevents us from appreciating the wide variation of educational opportunities offered by these schools, which vary greatly in the standards that they demand at entry, in staffing, the size of the sixth form and the quality of the teaching given. At one end are the public schools, many with a long history of first rate academic achievement. At the other are private schools which provide an indifferent education for the children of parents whose main aim is to preserve their social standing, and whose children might otherwise be on a non-academic course at a secondary modern school.

[52]

We have accordingly looked again at the achievement of these pupils after dividing them into those at public schools and other (non-public) independent and private.

'The fact is I do not know what a public school is. No one has been able to provide me with a satisfactory definition.' This confession of ignorance (quoted from Dancy 1963, p. 37) came from the Minister of Education in 1961 and certainly the term 'public school' means a number of different things to different people. Officially a boys' public school is one whose headmaster is a member of the Headmasters' Conference: in order to qualify for this, the school must be run by an independent governing body, the headmaster must enjoy some considerable degree of freedom in directing the educational policy of his school, and the academic standard of the pupils must reach a certain level. In 1966, there were 241 members of the Headmasters' Conference but not all their schools are independent—a few are grammar schools and roughly a third are direct grant. It is the pupils in the independent public schools that we shall be concerned with here.

In the past it has been fashionable to speak of the public schools as comprehensive. This is mistaken, for although there are some boys at public schools who have failed the 11+ examinations, they are in the minority. It is usual for public schools to have at least three boys of grammar school ability for every one below this level, whereas in a fully comprehensive school not more than one in four would be of this standard.

Impressive evidence of the effectiveness of teaching received in the public schools has been provided by Masters and Hockey (1963), who studied the records of boys who went to public schools after taking the 11+ examinations and failing to get grammar school places. 70 per cent gained five or more passes at 'O' level and over a quarter obtained two or more passes at 'A' level. Kalton's study and others at individual public schools have also produced similar findings, which illustrate that, given the opportunities provided at some schools, there is a large pool of talent to be developed.

Eighty-two boys in the National Survey were at public schools, most were boarders and their records, when measured in academic terms, are good compared with boys at other private schools. Their G.C.E. 'O' level results are better and they are more likely at each

[53]

level of ability to be still at school in 1962/3; in fact it is rare for a public school boy to leave before this. This late leaving is likely to give the public school boys an increasing advantage at a later age, for example those at the borderline level of ability do as well in their G.C.E. 'O' level examinations as the grammar school boys of similar ability, and as more of them, both with and without qualifications, remain at school to start the session 1962/3—whereas a large proportion of grammar school boys leave—they will certainly end up with a substantial advantage in their General Certificates.

Dancy (1963, page 45) attributes much of the success of the public school pupils to 'the tacit assumption that success at "O" level is within the capacity of everyone—and to the quality of the personal encouragement that is given such boys by all members of the staff who come into contact with them, especially their housemaster and their tutor'.

Peterson (quoted by Dancy, 1963, p. 60), writing with reference to university entrance, has said that the public school boy is fresher: 'Too often the grammar school sixth former, who leaves home at 8 and gets back at 5.30—with three hours of prep before him, is working too long a day for too many weeks in the year. If, as he normally does, he gives nine-tenths of that working time to three subjects only, most commonly physics, chemistry and mathematics, it is not surprising that he gets stale. If he repeats for a third year in the sixth very much the same syllabus that he did in his second year, it is not surprising that he gets staler still. All this the public school can largely avoid because of its better quality teachers, its better ratio of teachers to pupils and, most important, the fact that it is usually a boarding school.' Although this author is writing with reference to an older age group, his views are relevant also to the years we are studying.

The public schools are outstandingly successful in educating their pupils—but what of the boys at the independent and private schools which are not represented on the Headmasters' Conference? There are a few well known schools among these and National Survey boys at these schools have done well, though, on the average, the performance of the pupils at the non-member schools is below that expected from their ability. For example at the borderline level of ability, where this type of school might be expected to offer some special advantages, only 6 per cent gained good 'O' level certificates and only 50 per cent gained any certificate.* This compares with 29 per cent and 73 per cent of the grammar school boys. Pupils at these non-member schools leave much earlier than those at public schools and slightly earlier than those at grammar schools.

Seventy-three girls were at schools whose headmistresses were members of the Association of Headmistresses, but even in this group the girls of high ability have a disappointing record compared with the girls at grammar schools; this is in contrast with the less able who, although doing slightly less well in the General Certificate examination, stay on longer at school. Girls attending non-member schools achieve relatively little and leave early at all levels of ability.

We began this analysis by comparing the attainment and leaving age of those pupils in independent and private schools and those at grammar. We then went on to look at the middle class pupils in independent and private schools compared with all middle class pupils at all types of maintained school. The overall picture for 'O' level examination once ability is taken into account is, as we have seen, fairly favourable to the maintained schools: it is only at the highest level of ability that the boys at independent schools get consistently better certificates. It is apparent however that it is the pupils at independent schools who are the most likely to stay on at school to take 'A' levels, and possibly also repeat or add to their 'O' levels. While the examination performance of the boys at maintained schools up to sixteen is perhaps better than some might have realized, the picture for the girls is almost totally favourable to the maintained school pupils.

This chapter then went on to show that when the independent and private school pupils are divided according to their schools' membership of the Headmasters' Conference and Headmistresses' Association, attainment and age of leaving school differ sharply. The outstanding difference between the Headmasters' Conference and grammar school pupils lies in their leaving age. The girls at the Headmistresses' Association schools also, on the average, stay at school longer although their certificate results are not as good as those at grammar school.

Length of school life is, as we have seen in the previous chapters,

* See Table 15.

[55]

highly associated with social class; the more educated the parents, the longer their sons and daughters are likely to stay and the better they are likely to do at school. Any comparisons between the performance of pupils at different types of school should therefore take social class, as well as ability, into account, and it should also be remembered that the final examination level reached is, in itself, tied to length of school life.

To present tables comparing the final achievements of boys at Headmasters' Conference schools and all those at grammar schools, without reference to social class, is bound to highlight the better performance of those at independent schools; this is how Kalton presented his material. As however the background of pupils in the two types of school varies considerably, this is misleading, for it seems to infer that the differences are mainly due to different standards of teaching.

The difficulty is to find a group of boys at maintained schools with ability and parental background largely similar to those at the public schools. There were 90 boys at grammar schools from the upper middle class; 90 per cent of these boys started the session 1962/3, compared with 92 per cent of the Headmasters' Conference school boys.* Thus up to the threshold of the sixth form our evidence does not support Kalton's interpretation.

Lambert in the introduction to the Kalton report (1966) writes:

'As an organisation, the public school has a "total" approach. Its goals and values cover a wide range, both instrumentally and expressively, are explicit and stressed, are consciously apprehended by the community and deeply internalised. In directing its pupils towards those ends its scope is more all-embracing: it controls most of the pupil's time and activities and self-expression and caters for his most intimate necessities.'

Whether this 'total' approach brings about better academic achievement in the sixth form or not we shall wait to see.

We have been concerned with attainment only and have not touched on other aspects of training and experience received at school, many of which are not subject to measurement and assessment. Our summary must be that it is too soon yet to make a final judgment on the independent and private schools even at 'O' level,

* See Table 16.

for some pupils still at school, and particularly those at the large public schools, may be planning to sit this examination at a later age. These are the schools that are able to plan for a slower stream sitting 'O' levels one year later than is usual in the grammar schools, as well as an express stream taking them a year or more earlier— this is only possible in a school of a certain minimum size with a flexible organization. Indeed one of the advantages of the independent schools is that they are far freer than the maintained schools to try out new methods of organization and teaching.

Chapter Nine

Comprehensive Schools

It should be said at the outset that the following observations on the progress of pupils at comprehensive schools are far from satisfactory and point in conflicting directions. Some indicate that the comprehensive school pupils have an advantage over those at non-comprehensive maintained schools, while others show the reverse. These opposing answers probably stem from the limitations of the data at our disposal. In 1957 when the National Survey pupils transferred to their secondary schools, few local education authorities provided a wholly comprehensive system of education and the majority of the comprehensive schools then in existence were rigidly streamed: each was more like a combination of grammar, technical and secondary modern school, all existing under one headmaster, than a truly comprehensive school, with free transfer between streams, organized as a unit for pupils of the whole range of ability. In many areas moreover the comprehensive schools suffered from the diversion of able pupils to local grammar and direct grant schools. This meant that some schools, although nominally comprehensive, were little more than large secondary modern schools. These deficiencies were partly balanced however and sometimes more than balanced by the impetus given by the experimental nature of these enterprises; many were modern, splendidly equipped and staffed by exceptionally able and enthusiastic teachers.

A fair and balanced assessment of the relative value of a comprehensive and a selective system is clearly impossible in these circumstances, and would have been so even if there had been more than the small number of 280 National Survey pupils at comprehensive schools in England and Wales. We hope however that the following

[58]

observations will be helpful at a time when the Government's declared object is to end selection at 11+. The Government's intention is that when secondary education is organized on comprehensive lines, all that is valuable in grammar school education shall be preserved for those children who now receive it; moreover this type of academic education shall be made available to more pupils of a wider range of ability. In addition, it is intended that each pupil shall be given the opportunity and experience of mixing with others of all levels of attainment and from all kinds of home background. The local education authorities have accordingly been requested by the Secretary of State—in circular 10/65—to submit plans for re-organizing secondary education in their areas on comprehensive lines. As there is virtually no previous information to guide them, this is a difficult task, made even more difficult by the shortage of money for new buildings.

That the present selective system leads to unequal educational opportunity is clearly shown by the results of the National Survey. But these inequalities are, to a large extent, dependent on geographical differences which will not be removed simply by re-organizing existing schools on comprehensive lines: indeed re-organization, by hiding differences, may perpetuate them. One local authority for example appears now in official statistics* as an area in which more than 10 per cent of the thirteen year olds go to comprehensive schools and the fact that, on earlier lists, it was shown as providing grammar school places for less than 8 per cent of its pupils is forgotten.

While selection to the various types of secondary school is known to be socially biased except at the highest ranges of ability, there are other serious sources of inequality in the educational system—early streaming, for example, and the failure of many of the promising manual working class pupils to stay at school after the 'O' level examinations or indeed even to take them. In the grammar schools, strong pressures are exerted on an able pupil to stay on at school at least to the end of the fifth year and, even if his parents are uninterested and the neighbourhood antagonistic, a grammar school boy is likely to get some degree of support from his contemporaries which may encourage him to stay on. In spite of this, many lower manual

* List 69 of the Department of Education and Science.

[59]

working class pupils leave grammar school earlier than their teachers would wish, while others fail in their studies and are troublesome and unsettled at school. Some would explain this in terms of a conflict between the culture of the grammar schools and the culture of the homes, and would expect that the comprehensive schools, by diluting middle class values, might create a more nourishing educational environment for the manual working class pupils than the grammar schools are at present able to provide. It is however by no means certain that the able manual working class pupils are more favourably placed in comprehensive schools.

The values of the upper forms of comprehensive schools are likely to be as middle class in their ethos as those of the traditional grammar schools. For instance Holly (1965), writing of his findings in one comprehensive school, showed that those moving up streams were more than twice as likely to be middle as manual working class. It seems probable that the direction of movement of pupils between streams is, to a large extent, dependent on the help and interest that parents give their children with their homework. The middle class parents are better able to see what subjects their children are weak in and to arrange for extra tuition that may improve the standard of a weak subject and so raise their position in the school. Further, in a comprehensive school, the boy who starts in a relatively high position in his age group but fails to maintain it, may roll further and faster down the streams than if he had been at a grammar school, because he has farther to go. Discontented pupils, though not necessarily lacking in ability may, in this way, collect near the bottom of each year group to the detriment of the school. Owing to the larger size and full ability range in comprehensive schools, these pupils may present more of an educational problem than in either grammar or secondary modern schools.

Summing up the results of his study, Holly writes that social class 'seems to be a powerful variable in nearly all aspects of "profiting" from the school. Not only does it tend to dominate scholastic achievement in the sense of the "stream" structure but it is also an important factor in "late development". Those pupils—often quoted triumphantly by heads of comprehensive schools—who find themselves following Advanced sixth form courses, in spite of having been graded quite low in ability at 11+ tend to be drawn heavily from

[60]

favourable home backgrounds. Similarly, when allowance is made for sex-variations in attitude, it is middle class pupils who derive most from the activities provided by the school outside the curriculum, while middle class pupils are disproportionately represented among those fifth-formers who are chosen as prefects—less a function of teacher-bias, probably, than of school-centredness on the part of these young people themselves.'

These comments underline some of the major areas of uncertainty about comprehensive education. The limited information available from the National Survey, though it cannot provide more than a tentative answer to any of the questions that have been posed, provides an opportunity for two comparisons. First, the pupils at comprehensive schools are contrasted with those of similar measured ability at grammar, technical and secondary modern schools. Second, the pupils at schools in areas which provide a substantial proportion of comprehensive school places are contrasted with those in areas which are predominantly selective. These comparisons however may well miss aspects of comprehensive education that are of social or developmental importance, for as we have already pointed out, we are able to use at this stage only academic measures of achievement.

Of the fifteen year old pupils, 134 boys and 146 girls were at comprehensive schools in England and Wales. These are small numbers though larger than reported four years earlier when the group entered their secondary schools. Nearly a third of those who were at comprehensive schools at fifteen had started at eleven in secondary modern schools which later changed their designation either with or without re-organization. Apart from these renamed schools, the comprehensives are a mixed group. Some were bi-lateral schools and called themselves so: in these, modern and grammar (or technical) streams were housed in the same buildings. Others, though not bi-lateral in name, divided their pupils by ability into academic and non-academic streams. Many of these schools were in areas that also had selective schools, so that they were sometimes deprived of the ablest boys and girls and therefore of the possibility of establishing and sustaining an effective sixth form. All that can be said of the so called comprehensive schools in this study is that they represent varying efforts at providing, within one organization, education for pupils of a wide though in most instances not a complete range of ability. The distribution of test scores among fifteen year old pupils at comprehensive schools is as expected; there are fewer boys and girls of high ability than in the maintained schools as a whole. A rather higher proportion of girls than of boys go to comprehensive schools; on the other hand, there is a rather greater deficit of able girls than of able boys among the comprehensive school pupils.

The comprehensive schools, in this Survey, are on the average larger than the other maintained schools, have better and newer buildings, are less crowded, have smaller classes and superior laboratories, art rooms, workshops and other amenities. The proportion of graduates on their staff is the same as for the other maintained schools, though the headmasters of the comprehensive schools report more shortages of mathematics and science teachers. This may well arise from different standards since the headmasters of comprehensive schools take into account the needs of pupils at all levels of ability, whereas the heads of grammar and secondary modern schools focus their attention on the needs of pupils of a more restricted range. The re-organization of secondary education on comprehensive lines is not likely to decrease the demand for highly qualified staff.

The pupils at comprehensive schools are described as coming from families of similar cultural backgrounds to those in the other maintained schools, though there is a slight deficiency of upper middle class pupils. When comparing comprehensive pupils with those at other maintained schools, allowances have to be made for measured ability; if this was not done, the other maintained schools would have an illusory advantage arising from the higher ability of their pupils. The comprehensive school pupils at each level of ability below 60—in the fifteen year tests—are less likely than those of similar ability at the other maintained schools to leave at the earliest opportunity and are more likely to complete the session 1961/2. It is particularly those of around average ability from the manual working classes who seem to benefit, whereas the middle class pupils show the same pattern of leaving in each type of school. In contrast, the pupils of high ability leave comprehensive schools at an earlier age than those of similar ability in other maintained schools. This may be owing to the lack of tradition and facilities available in the schools that have already been deprived of their most able pupils by the surrounding grammar schools; or perhaps the two groups of able pupils are not comparable—those at the other maintained schools including more very able boys and girls.

Exactly similar conclusions are reached when the proportions gaining one or more 'O' level passes in the General Certificate of Education examinations are compared. The pupils of high ability are more likely to be successful in the other maintained schools, whereas the less able pupils at each level of ability below 60 are more likely to be successful if they are at comprehensive schools, though the differences here are small and statistically not significant.

A different picture is given when the pupils' own views on further education are examined. Those at comprehensive schools are less prepared than those at other maintained schools to continue with full-time higher education after leaving school—this is most marked for the pupils of high ability where this type of education has a more precise meaning, because the majority will at least have considered the possibility of entering the universities or colleges of education. Again this may reflect the higher ability of the able boys and girls in the other maintained schools; against this however should be set the fact that both the teachers and the mothers of the pupils at comprehensive schools take views of the abilities of the boys and girls which are closely similar to those of the teachers and mothers of the pupils of high ability at the other maintained schools. It is the boys and girls themselves who differ in their aspirations and they do so dramatically. Only 29 per cent of the comprehensive school pupils of high ability wish to continue with full-time higher education after leaving school, compared with 60 per cent of the pupils at other maintained schools. How real this difference is, will be seen at the later stages of this inquiry, when we know how many fulfil the intentions they expressed at fifteen.

The problem of the selective diversion of the more able pupils to grammar schools is avoided if, instead of comparing the comprehensive school pupils with those at other types of school, the performance of all pupils in areas with many comprehensive school places is compared with that of all pupils in areas with few. At the time of this study, a number of local education authorities provided a substantial proportion of comprehensive school places for their

[63]

pupils. In 1959, there were 26 local education authorities in England and Wales whose comprehensive provision was between 10 and 100 per cent.* 600 pupils in the educational sample were at schools within their boundaries. The ages of leaving and the proportion of pupils gaining good certificates are exactly the same in these 26 areas as elsewhere in England and Wales but the lower manual working class pupils are at a disadvantage—only 1·7 of them get good certificates compared with 5·3 per cent of the lower manual working class pupils in other areas. While this suggests that the lower manual working class pupils may be handicapped in comprehensive schools, it should be remembered that the local education authority areas with a high proportion of comprehensive school places include many rural authorities and this, rather than the comprehensive policy which they follow, may explain the poorer performance of the lower manual working class.

An observational study, even in the best circumstances, cannot lead to a firm conclusion on the relative merits of the two educational systems. An opportunity for experiment is needed in which comprehensive education is fostered in some areas and selective education in others, the areas chosen being equivalent in social composition and educational opportunity. It is probably too late now however to set up such experiments; the pace of development and change is too fast.

The observations reported in this chapter give no clear indications of the strengths and weaknesses of the comprehensive schools. They provide some evidence that even in the late 1950s these schools were fulfilling the hopes of their founders in encouraging the manual working class pupils to remain longer at school and to take the General Certificate of Education. On the other hand they also provide evidence that aspirations for further education may be dampened in the comprehensive schools. It may be felt that, in our assessments, insufficient attention has been paid to the progress of the average pupil who in particular might be expected to benefit from comprehensive education—this, as has been explained, was unavoidable. The schools we have described are moreover an exceptional group and no general conclusions can or should be drawn. We can only recognize the difficulties of assessing compre-

* See List 69 of the Department of Education and Science.

hensive education and the dangers of changing to a comprehensive system before adequate information exists to show how the new schools should be planned.

The fact that inequalities existed within the old selective system does not mean that they will disappear when selective examinations are abolished; and the fact that it is the pupils from poor homes who have been handicapped in the past, does not necessarily mean that they will lose these handicaps when comprehensive education becomes universal. Perhaps more rather than less attention will be needed to enable the able boy or girl from a deprived home to use to the full the opportunities offered by his comprehensive school.

Chapter Ten

Co-education

While the majority of middle class parents prefer to educate their sons and daughters in separate schools, this is by no means a universal attitude. Some see co-education as more 'natural'—though more in the social than in the educational sense—and many teachers see the girls as exerting a civilizing influence on the boys. Recent interviews with Survey members now at the universities give the views of some of the abler pupils who had themselves been at co-educational schools. A girl refers to the difficulties of being educated with boys:

'I was with boys for two years; it was difficult communicating things. They used to try and embarrass me as much as possible, which was very awkward, but they were very good, and very helpful; anything I couldn't do they used to come and do for me, and I used to go out hiking with them.'

Another girl sets out the advantages:

'. . . I think all girls together must be frightful—bitchiness and this sort of thing which the boys in our form tended to relieve us of . . . two sexes in a class add something in discussions . . . you've had some sort of working relationship with people of the opposite sex . . . a very valuable relationship . . . and nice friendships.'

And a boy, also from a co-educational school, puts the educational advantages:

'There is a great danger in single sex schools of thinking that girls are inferior and that you can't honestly expect a girl to argue . . . I think if you did come up to university still thinking this, you would be in for rather a shock.'

A boy from a single sex school took an ambivalent attitude:

[66]

'I think there are advantages in a single sex school. I think you can work better without girls. But I am beginning to realize now at university, as there are girls in our class, that it doesn't make much difference really.'

Finally, the lack of social maturity that may go with segregated schooling was noted by a boy who had himself been at a co-educational school:

'I found the girls who have been at girls' schools only, when they get to university, absolutely break out. The first term was absolutely hectic, girls were flying around, absolutely scatter-brained. I was quite astounded.'

In the discussions we had with university students on the education of boys and girls the majority of criticisms were aimed at single sex schools. The few that were directed at co-educational schools came from those who had had no first-hand experience of them. This also appears to be true of their teachers (Dale, 1955, 1965); those who have worked in both types of school largely favour the co-educational.

We now turn to the evidence provided by the National Survey. Our aim is to compare mixed and single sex schools and their pupils, without attempting to argue a case either for or against co-education.

In 1959, 46 per cent of the pupils in this sample were in mixed classes and two years later the proportion had risen to 49 per cent— a small trend, perhaps, but one that is likely to continue, owing to the difficulty of recruiting adequately trained and experienced staff to the girls' schools. It is not unusual to hear of sixth-form girls visiting the local boys' schools for special tuition, usually in science, and with the increasing numbers studying to take their 'A' levels, it seems that this practice may well spread. Evidence of the acute shortage of women teachers also comes from the staff rooms of mixed secondary schools. It might be expected that men and women would be equally represented in these schools but, in fact, the proportion of men teachers far exceeds that of women. The wastage rate of women teachers is high in all types of school—many are employed for a short time only before marriage and starting a family and this of course means both a high turn-over and many inexperienced teachers in the girls' schools.

[67]

Mixed schools, although found in all parts of England and Wales,* are more common in the rural areas. Historically of course this has always been so. Boys and girls in the villages went to the local school that catered for all children and, although the 'all-age' school is now almost a thing of the past, re-organization has not meant separate education for many of these country boys and girls for among other things this would be uneconomical; a school must be a certain minimum size for efficiency. While there are pupils in mixed secondary schools in all parts of England and Wales, co-education is not found equally in all regions. The highest proportion of National Survey pupils in mixed schools was in Wales and the North. Sixty-five per cent of the Welsh boys and girls were in mixed classes and 62 per cent of the Northern; this compared with 38 per cent in the South-East and 39 per cent in the North-West. It was relatively rare to find pupils at mixed independent and direct grant schools although 36 per cent of those at grammar schools were at co-educational ones. The highest proportion in mixed classes, within any type of school, is found at the secondary modern and comprehensive schools.

Just over half the manual working class pupils were at co-educational schools, as compared with only two-fifths of the lower middle class and one-quarter of the upper middle class pupils, a difference that is in part explained by the high proportion of middle class pupils in the segregated grammar schools. It seems however that in addition to this, if given the choice, middle class parents are more likely to choose a segregated than a co-educational school. Why this should be is uncertain, but no doubt the past academic records of the schools, traditional attitudes and the upbringing of the parents themselves all help to shape a preference for one type of school rather than another. And it is the middle class parents who are mobile and more in a position to choose the district in which they live and so the type of school to which their children go.

To try to assess the academic progress of those in co-education, we consider only pupils at grammar or secondary modern schools. The number of independent, direct grant, technical and comprehensive school pupils are too small to warrant any special comparisons.

* Owing to the higher proportion of Scottish pupils attending co-educational schools, the comparisons in this chapter are limited to England and Wales.

There were 269 boys and girls in mixed grammar schools and 949 in mixed secondary modern throughout their years at secondary school; it is these schools and their pupils that are compared with the single sex schools.

The pupils in segregated grammar schools were in smaller classes than those in mixed. More of their class-mates were from middle class homes (especially the girls) and the average leaving ages for both sexes were higher than in the mixed grammar schools. More of the boys were at schools which were large, had a high proportion of graduates on the staff and had relatively few teaching vacancies. The girls' schools, in comparison, were smaller than the mixed, and fewer graduates and more teaching vacancies. More of the mixed than of the single sex schools were in rural areas, and more of the headmasters of the mixed schools complained about the buildings.

The characteristics of the secondary modern schools, grouped once again by type of school attended by members of the Survey, show similar staffing differences. The boys' schools had the most highly qualified teachers and fewest staff vacancies, followed by the mixed schools and finally the girls. The segregated schools were nearly all in urban areas. In the secondary modern schools the headmasters of the segregated schools were more likely to complain of the buildings.

So much for the characteristics of the schools. Let us now turn to the educational progress of the pupils. For the following comparisons it is necessary that the boys and girls should be grouped not only by whether they are at single or mixed sex schools, but also by their family backgrounds; for middle class parents, and especially the upper middle class, in general prefer to send their children to single sex schools, and these boys and girls on the whole stay at school the longest and make the best progress.

Of the test results two questions may be asked. First, what, if any, was the difference in average performance of pupils entering the single and mixed secondary schools, and second, how has their performance in tests changed during the subsequent four years? Only the results of the reading and mathematics test which were given at eleven and fifteen years are referred to here.

At eleven years the boys who are about to enter single sex grammar schools are superior in both reading and arithmetic to those going

[69]

to the mixed grammar schools. This holds for pupils from both social classes and is probably due partly to parental choice—the parents of the more able choosing the grammar schools of higher standing which tend to be for boys only—and partly because the segregated grammar schools are able to demand a higher standard at entry. The middle class at boys' grammar schools are in both mathematics and reading relatively further ahead of their opposite numbers in mixed grammar schools at fifteen years, than at eleven. This is also true of manual working class boys for reading; in mathematics and arithmetic, although they were still comfortably ahead of those at mixed sex grammar schools, at fifteen their advantage was less than four years earlier. It seems then that the abler boys are more likely to go to single than to mixed sex grammar schools, and once there, maintain or increase their initial superiority in attainment.

In the secondary modern schools in arithmetic and reading tests the boys in segregated, are slightly below those in mixed classes at eleven. During the subsequent four years however they show a relative improvement in both types of tests, so that at fifteen there is little difference between the average scores in the two types of school, single or mixed.

The middle class girls in mixed grammar schools are superior at entry to those in girls' grammar schools in the tests of both reading and arithmetic, and by fifteen years they have increased their lead. The findings for the manual working class girls however are different. Those going to segregated grammar schools make higher scores at eleven in both reading and arithmetic than those going to the mixed schools; it seems that manual working class girls have to achieve a higher standard for a place in a girls' grammar school, than would be required for a place in a mixed grammar school. The gap between the test performance of the manual working class girls in the two types of grammar school has narrowed in reading by fifteen years, so that those taught in mixed schools, who were behind at eleven years, have partly caught up with those in the girls' schools. In the mixed secondary modern schools the girls made relatively better progress in reading and mathematics than in the single sex schools and the middle class girls in particular were at an advantage.

We turn now to achievement in the General Certificate of Education 'O' level examinations and to the average leaving ages from each type of school. The middle class boys stay longer at school and gain more good certificates if they go to single rather than to mixed sex grammar or secondary modern schools. In contrast, middle class girls at single sex grammar and secondary modern schools leave earlier than those at mixed. They also have fewer good certificates and are less likely to wish to carry on with their studies after leaving school.

The middle class boys at both grammar and secondary modern schools are consistently more favourably placed than the middle class girls in attainment, leaving pattern, G.C.E. results and aspirations for higher education, but this is only so if comparisons are limited to single sex schools. In the mixed schools the girls are assessed as favourably as the boys; even in mathematics they are only slightly below the boys in performance, while in reading they are superior; they also stay as long at school as the boys and are as likely to get good 'O' levels. Looked at in another way, these results show that middle class girls at mixed schools reach higher educational standards than middle class girls in single sex schools. But the reverse holds for the middle class boys, who are at an advantage in the single sex schools.

A different picture emerges for the manual working class pupils. There are no significant differences in the achievement of boys and girls at single sex grammar schools. The girls stay on rather longer than the boys, but the boys get rather more good certificates. Similar proportions of the boys and girls at these single sex schools intend to continue with full-time study after leaving school. In the mixed grammar schools both manual working class boys and girls have low levels of achievement, tend to leave early and have low aspirations for further education.

Why should the pattern of the manual working class be different from that of middle class pupils? And why should manual working class pupils at mixed schools achieve the least? Part of the answer lies no doubt in initial selection; the segregated schools select the more able manual working class pupils, especially the girls, and once there, these pupils will be under pressure to conform to the middle class values of the schools, considerable stress being laid on homework and hard work. In the secondary modern schools such

[71]

pressures will be lighter, and perhaps owing to this the performance of manual working class boys and girls is similar, whether they are at single or mixed secondary modern schools.

A clear-cut comparison between the performance of pupils at single sex and co-educational schools is not possible, because the effects of the school depend on the home background and sex of the pupil. The middle class boys and all the manual working class boys and girls at grammar schools stay on longer and get better 'O' level results if they are at single sex schools. On the other hand, as already indicated, middle class girls are at a considerable advantage in the mixed sex schools. In the secondary modern schools also, the middle class girls stay on longer in the mixed schools, whereas the middle class boys and all the manual working class pupils have a similar pattern of leaving whether they are at single or mixed sex schools.

In the secondary schools the pupils show a wide range of sexual maturity and this is an appropriate point to discuss whether there are any advantages or disadvantages for the early maturing boy or girl in co-educational schools. The boys who come early into puberty stay on the longest in each type of school, but the early maturing girls in each social class are only more likely to stay on if they are at a mixed school. At the single sex girls' schools, 32 per cent of the early maturing girls do not start the 1962/3 session compared with only 19 per cent of the late maturers.* It is likely that the explanation lies in the increasing resentment of these advanced girls at being treated as school children.

There has been no previous study of co-education based on a national sample but the few local studies that have been made (Dale, 1962) show that boys in co-educational schools were more successful in passing examinations than boys in single sex schools; no account however was taken of those pupils not sitting the examinations. Our own evidence is at variance with this, perhaps because the majority of these studies were made 30 to 40 years ago and the nature of co-education has probably changed considerably since then.

There are it seems both advantages and disadvantages about co-education but our information is insufficient to explain why this should be. Do middle class girls thrive in co-educational schools because

* See Table 17.

[72]

they find it easier to learn from masters than mistresses, and could similar standards have been achieved by masters in girls' schools? Do girls in co-educational schools suffer from being directed into narrowly conventional courses because of the biases of their head-masters, who are perhaps more ready than headmistresses would be to accept domestic or clerical studies as the most suitable for girls, perhaps just because they are clearly unsuitable for boys? Or the reverse might be true, the girls benefiting from the better science and mathematics teaching in co-educational schools. The evidence of the Crowther Report (1959) (Table 49, page 253) suggests that at the sixth form level there is a greater tendency for the boys to do science and the girls to do arts in the co-educational schools. Or again, do the girls in co-educational schools lose their freedom to develop as individuals because they are forced at an early age to conform to the expectations of a mixed teenage culture? These are important questions, outside the scope of this Survey, which need answering before we drift, without intention, into creating a system of mixed comprehensive schools.

Chapter Eleven

Regional Differences in Educational Opportunity and Attainment

In the secondary school years few of the families, only 4 per cent, moved across regional boundaries. The boys and girls from these families were of rather higher ability and attainment than those who either remained at the same address or, if they moved, stayed within the same region. This was also true for the children of the families who moved during the pre- and early school years. As so few families moved across regional boundaries between 1957 and 1961, they have been excluded from the following regional description which refers only to the 96 per cent who remained throughout the secondary school years in the same region.

Secondary schools in Scotland differ in many ways from those in England and Wales. Selection occurs a year later, there are no technical and relatively few independent or grant-aided schools; the pupils are allocated to either senior secondary five-year or junior secondary three-year courses at 12+. In a number of schools, particularly those rurally situated, both types of courses are frequently provided under the same roof. The five-year courses in Scotland correspond roughly to the grammar and technical school courses south of the border, but more pupils take them—in this study 38 per cent in Scotland compared with 30 per cent in England and Wales were on academic courses of all kinds. The greater provision of selective, or grammar school type, academic courses in Scotland almost certainly eases pressures in the top classes of the Scottish primary schools; strains do no doubt exist at this age in Scotland and are more intense in some schools and some areas than in others, but on the whole they are probably less intense than in England and Wales. At earlier ages the influences in the two countries are reversed, for there is evidence that Scottish children, the middle class in particular, are under heavy pressures during the early years at primary school.

The attainment of eight year old Scottish pupils is, on the whole, superior to that of pupils in England and Wales, and it is in the reading test that they have the greatest advantage. By eleven years the English and Welsh pupils have nearly caught up with the Scots in reading and surpassed them in vocabulary; in arithmetic, however the Scots are superior, as they also are in mathematics at fifteen. The Scottish pupils make low scores in all the non-verbal intelligence tests, an observation that confirms the recent findings of a study comparing the test results of pupils in 12 countries, including Scotland (UNESCO, 1962). In the aggregate scores for all tests at eight the Scots are nearly one point ahead of the English and Welsh; this is a substantial and significant advantage, but it has vanished by the age of eleven and has not reappeared at fifteen.

The Scots at each level of ability and in each social class have a greater chance of following a selective course—indeed the manual working class pupil in Scotland is as likely to be on a selective course as the middle class pupil in England and Wales of the same level of ability. There are social inequalities in secondary selection in both countries, though they are greater in England and Wales possibly owing to the part played by the independent schools.

Very early leaving is rather more common in Scotland than in England and Wales, though the proportion still at school at the beginning of the 1962/3 session is the same; this slight excess of early leavers may reflect the more difficult employment situation in Scotland.*

Scottish 'O' level examinations were sat for the first time in 1962, the normal time of preparation being four years; thus the members of the National Survey were among the first to take them. (In earlier years 'lowers' were taken at the same time as 'highers', usually at seventeen years of age.) How the standard of 'O' level papers and marking in Scotland compares with that of the various boards south of the border is not known, though the results in terms of good 'O' levels and the proportion getting certificates both suggest that the overall standards are similar. Rather more boys in Scotland leave

* See Table 18.

[75]

without a certificate at all, but this is partly owing to the heavier early fall-out from school. It seems therefore that 'O' level examination results are roughly parallel in the two countries, in spite of different educational opportunities and different ages of transfer, though it is of course too early to make a final assessment of the two systems. The Scots have a tradition that the way to the universities is open to any able pupil whatever his social class or economic circumstances, and they may be aiming higher than the English or the Welsh, although so far we have no evidence of this. A rather higher proportion of Scottish than of English or Welsh boys said they hoped to continue with full-time education after leaving, but equal proportions of girls.

Comparisons between the English and Welsh pupils are impracticable because there are only 184 Welsh pupils in the educational sample. Impracticable also is a detailed regional analysis within England, for numbers are too small. A simple division of England into North and South by a line running roughly from the Wash to the Bristol Channel yields however some interesting comparisons. Historically this line separates the country into two nations, the Northern having a high infant and maternal death rate and poor living conditions, and the Southern a low death rate and better living conditions. These differences hold to some extent today.

Of the Survey families living in the North of England 18 per cent were middle class compared with 30 per cent of those in the South. It is not unexpected therefore to find that the level of measured ability is higher and the results of the 'O' level examinations are better in the South. Once comparisons are made between similar social classes however there are no differences in the verbal and non-verbal intelligence test scores at fifteen and none in mathematics, but the pupils in the South—particularly the manual working class —make rather higher scores in reading.

The proportions of pupils going to grammar schools in the two regions are similar, but the South has the benefit of more technical and independent schools, so that when these are included 4 per cent more of the Southern pupils get a selective education. In each social class those from the South stay on longer at school, fewer leave early and more enter the session 1962/3 than in the North. They also achieve more in the 'O' level examinations, though here it should be remembered that there are nine examination boards whose standards are thought to vary, and this may lead to differences between the two regions. At each level of ability however the Southern pupils get more good certificates than the Northern and fewer leave without any certificate. There were no differences in the proportion who expressed the intention of entering higher education after leaving school, but discrepancies are to be expected later when actual 'A' levels and university entry are known. We anticipate that similar proportions will go on to higher education but that a greater proportion of the Southerners will go to the universities.

If grammar school pupils in the North are compared with grammar school pupils in the South the same differences in leaving and examination results appear though they are rather less marked. When those at secondary modern schools are considered, similar differences between North and South are also found.

If, as we suspect, a considerable part of the social inequalities in educational opportunity are a result of the patchy distribution of selective schools, it would be logical to group the local education authorities by the proportion of pupils sent to grammar and other selective schools, rather than by geographical location. Grouped in this way, it should be possible to see whether areas which are relatively deficient in selective school places are providing additional facilities for pupils in non-selective schools to take courses leading to the G.C.E. examinations. The wide range of provision that is made for pupils on selective courses in the different local education authorities is shown in List 69 published by the Department of Education and Science, and this list has been used to group the local education authorities in England and Wales by the proportion of thirteen year old pupils who were in grammar, technical, direct grant or independent schools in 1959. Scottish schools are excluded. After removing all authorities with 10 per cent or more of their pupils at comprehensive schools, the local education authorities are divided into the following three groups.

(a) Those with few places—13 to 23 per cent of pupils in
    Selective schools;
(b) Those with average number of places—24 to 25 per cent;
(c) Those with many places—26 to 36 per cent.

[77]

The local education authorities which provide 24 per cent or more of their pupils with selective education tend to be concentrated in the South of England, and in both North and South they serve areas where a high proportion of middle class families are found. In the rural and in the largely manual working class districts selective school places are in shorter supply. The age of school buildings and the provision of laboratories and workrooms is remarkably similar in the three groups of local education authorities, but there are considerable differences in the staffing of the schools. Local education authorities which send 26 per cent or more of their pupils to selective schools have a higher proportion of graduate staff and fewer staff shortages. Some of these differences in staffing arise from the higher proportion of selective schools in these areas, though this is not the only explanation as they persist when comparisons are between the grammar schools only, or between the secondary modern schools only. For example, in the areas with many places, 30 per cent of the headmasters of grammar schools with Survey pupils complained of shortages of staff compared with 42 per cent of those in areas with few.

The parents of the manual working class boys and girls in the areas with many places appear to take a greater interest in their school work, whether this is estimated by the schools' assessments of interest or by the number of times their fathers visited the schools to discuss their sons' or daughters' progress with the heads or form teachers. As the teachers in the areas where there are many grammar school places are likely to have higher standards in their assessments of parental interest than those in the areas with few, the differences observed may well underestimate the real ones. This association of high parental interest with plentiful provision of grammar school places is not limited to any social class, for it is evident among the parents of both grammar and secondary modern school pupils. The fact that many selective school places are supplied in an area may reflect the interest taken locally in education. On the other hand education itself is infectious and the more places that are supplied the more the parents become aware of the importance of learning.

Once account has been taken of the fact that there are more middle class pupils in the areas which provide many selective school places, there are relatively small differences in the average test results between those living in the three types of authority. Boys in the areas with 26 per cent or more selective school places have a slight, but statistically not significant advantage in each group of tests over boys in areas with few places. The girls however show a different pattern. At eight years, the groups are of approximately the same average level of ability, but later they progressively diverge so that those in the areas with many selective school places make scores that are increasingly above those in areas with few. Thus, in the best provided areas the girls do nearly as well as the boys in the tests and the difference between them is not statistically significant, whereas in the areas with few places they do considerably less well. These area differences hold for each test, though in all areas the girls do relatively poorly in mathematics compared with the boys.

Pupils stay at school longest in the local education authorities which provide the most selective school places. In these areas 59 per cent stayed on after the minimum leaving age compared with 44 per cent in the areas with few places. These differences are found both for the boys and girls and for middle and manual working class pupils, at all levels of ability apart from the highest: few of the pupils of high ability leave at an early age in any of the three groups of areas.

There are similar differences between the three areas in G.C.E. results. Where there are many selective school places 27 per cent of the pupils gained a certificate of some kind by the age of sixteen and a half compared with 23 per cent of those in areas with few.* Parallel differences are found for both boys and girls and for middle and manual working class pupils. When standards are raised however and only those who gained a good certificate at 'O' level are considered, these differences vanish and, as with leaving, it seems that for the boys and girls of high ability, who in any area would reach a grammar school, the availability of selective school places has no demonstrable effect.

A further and probably more realistic estimate of the influence of the supply of selective school places on the educational performance of pupils is given by the proportion starting the session 1962/3.

* See Table 19.

[79]

Here also there are marked differences between the three groups of local education authorities. When there are few selective school places only 19 per cent stay on, whereas when there are many places 30 per cent do so. These differences are greatest for the manual working class pupils, particularly the girls, only 12 per cent of whom remain at school to start the 1962/3 session when there are few places, whereas 21 per cent stay on when there are many.

The conclusions from this account of regional differences in Great Britain are that, although the Scottish system of education is very different from that south of the border, the final outcome is remarkably similar—differences in pressures, in the provision of selective courses and in the age of transfer do not materially alter the final result. For generations the Scots have lost some of their ablest members through emigration, and yet on the average the Scottish child is, in both measured intelligence and examination performance, as able as the English and it might be argued, and supported by the results of the non-verbal intelligence tests, that this reflects a superior educational system acting on a depleted population.

In England and Wales itself there are considerable regional differences on either side of the line dividing the country from the Wash to the Bristol Channel. These differences are in a sense historical and are reflected in a whole variety of other attributes such as mortality and standards of living as well as in the provision of independent and technical schools.

That the patchy distribution of grammar schools throughout the country leads to unequal educational opportunity is shown by a comparison of the performance of pupils in the areas of local educational authorities which provide many, or few, selective school places. In test performance the picture is that the girls in the authorities with few places do progressively less well, falling behind the boys, whereas in the areas where there are many places they do nearly as well as the boys. In leaving and in the results of the G.C.E. examinations also the data show that increasing the proportion of selective school places leads to better performance; this holds for boys as well as for girls and for all social classes.

Part III

Parents and Children

Chapter Twelve

Some Characteristics of the Parents

There is much evidence in the earlier chapters of the importance of the support and encouragement that parents give their children with their school work. At the primary stage the level of parental interest is a major factor in school success, and for many of the able boys and girls it is a decisive element at fifteen or sixteen years when they choose whether to stay on at school, and later when they choose whether or not to enter higher education. We are impressed by the consistency of the assessments of parental attitudes throughout the early lives of these boys and girls. The mothers who, during the school years, took little interest in their children's work include a high proportion of those who were described earlier by the health visitors as being poor managers in looking after their homes and children. Further, there is a similarity in the assessments of school interest made during the primary and secondary school years. Few of those reported as giving their children little encouragement with their work at primary school are more favourably assessed at the secondary stage.

Perhaps the best evidence of the stability of parental attitudes is given by the fact that the average differences in test score and in school performance between the most favourably and least favourably assessed families is similar, whether the pupils are grouped by the standard of care given in infancy, or by the level of interest shown by their parents in their school work at secondary school.

It seems that, generally speaking, the schools are failing to involve some parents in the process of their children's education. There are, no doubt, many individual instances in which unenthusiastic or distrustful fathers and mothers have, after discussion with the head and other teachers, been led to appreciate the value of education for their children. Many boys and girls however even some who are succeeding at school and manifestly benefiting from the teaching they are receiving, have parents who take little interest in their work.

There is no need to enlarge further on the relevance of parental interest and its implications. High interest is closely linked to high attainment, good results in the 'O' level examination and long school life in the next generation, whereas low interest is associated with poor performance and early leaving. This is true not only of the population as a whole, but also when each social class is considered separately. We shall look now at the extent to which the parents' attitudes to school work and hopes for their children's future employment, are related to their own age and education.

In *The Home and the School* it was shown that the views of the parents on when their children should leave school were unrelated to their own age. In the upper middle class, the oldest fathers wished to keep their children longest at school, in the other social classes the youngest. All differences were however small. From this it was argued that parents of all ages, however distant their own schooling, are equally affected by current views on the value of a longer school life for their children. This conclusion can now be examined in greater depth using the additional information collected during the secondary school years.

The sample of boys and girls in the National Survey is based on the births occurring during a certain week; thus families were not selected by either marriage date or the age of the parents. The ages of the parents do in fact cover a wide range; some of the fathers and a few of the mothers were at school before the First World War whereas others were still at school during the Second. With these great differences of age and hence educational experience it would have been reasonable to expect the younger rather than the older parents to have higher aspirations for their children and to give them more support and encouragement in their work; but this is found neither when the boys and girls are classified separately by the age of each parent, nor when the ages of both parents are considered together. To avoid repetition the combined ages are used here.

It is convenient to divide the families into those in which both

[84]

parents were under thirty at the birth of the Survey child, those in which one was over thirty, and those in which both were over thirty. As the middle class parents are older on the average than the manual working class, the social groups have to be considered separately. There is no close or consistent relationship between parental age and level of interest, although older middle class parents take a greater interest in their daughters' education than the younger. This difference is in the opposite direction to that expected. For manual working class boys and girls and for middle class boys there is no suggestion of either an increase or decrease in interest among the older parents.

Neither attitude to work nor school absence is related to parental age, although the greater amount of illness recorded for the older parents (see Chapter XIII) implies that their children should lose more time from school. Similarly test scores, 'O' level results and age of leaving school are independent of parental age, and roughly equal proportions of parents in each of these groups hope that their children will continue with full-time higher education after leaving school.

These findings confirm the earlier conclusion reached in *The Home and the School* that parents' views on the education of their children and their children's attainment are similar whatever their age. It seems that parents, irrespective of when they themselves were at school, have the opinions and standards that are current at the time their own children are being educated. Presumably when the elder brothers and sisters of the Survey children were at school, some in the 1930's and many in the 1940's, their parents' aspirations were lower, being set at a level appropriate to the more restricted educational opportunities that were then available. This is an unexpected conclusion because if, as some feel, education is an infectious process, then those who have benefited from the improved education of recent years should have been the ones to show the greatest appreciation of the value of education for their own children.

The importance of education in the older generation is well illustrated by the fathers who had been brought up in manual working class families. The social and occupational status of these men in middle age is closely related to the education they received. The chances of reaching non-manual employment were small for

[85]

those whose education had ceased before fifteen, and the 5 per cent who did become non-manual workers were mainly employed as travellers, shop assistants, non-commissioned officers, policemen, etc., jobs that have, on the whole, relatively few middle class characteristics. Any effort at further education on the part of the ex-elementary school pupils was associated with improved chances of upward social movement, the extent of this movement being directly related to the standard achieved. Thus of those who had been to elementary schools and made no attempt to get further education, 93 per cent were employed in manual work, compared with 68 per cent of those who on leaving elementary school had taken some further course leading to a higher qualification.

Education beyond the elementary level greatly improved the chances of men with working class origins entering middle class occupations. For example only 18 per cent of those who went to secondary school and later took some form of further education that gave them a diploma or degree remained in manual occupations in which their fathers had spent their working lives, while 42 per cent entered the professions. Education, in addition, widened their social contacts; they were more likely to marry women who also had a superior education, and they were more likely to marry into the middle classes. In contrast very few of those whose education ceased when they left elementary school married wives with a better education than themselves, or from a superior social background. Thus the effects of education on social movement are reinforced by marriage, and this in turn influences opportunities of social advancement in the succeeding generation. It is evident from the job histories of these men during the Survey years that marriage to women with superior education or from the middle classes confers stability on their own employment pattern and acts as an insurance against downward social movement. It is also associated with superior educational opportunities for their children.

In the manual working classes assessments of parental interest tie up closely with the education that the parents themselves have had. The main difference is between those with only elementary school education and the rest. Any attempt to improve education beyond the elementary school level, whether by night classes or by correspondence courses, is associated with an increase in the level

[86]

of interest taken in their children's education.* Thus for the mothers the level of interest taken by those who only had elementary school education but tried to get further education after leaving school, is approximately as high as for those with secondary education or better.

Similar conclusions are reached if instead of taking the estimates of the parents' interest we look at the views of the mothers on the higher education of their children.† Fifty-three per cent of the manual working class parents who were at elementary school only and had no further study, later wish their children to continue with full-time education after leaving school, compared with 71 per cent of those who had themselves been to the same type of school but had tried to improve their education by further study.

It has been reported by other workers (e.g. Deutsch and Brown, 1964) that children whose fathers are frequently away or absent from home are likely to fall behind the rest in school performance. This can be examined in the present study where, in addition to obtaining information about broken families, the health visitors asked at intervals whether the father's work often kept him away from home for 48 hours or more. The total number of fathers who were frequently away from home was relatively small, 330, and of these only 118 were consistently away throughout the years their children were at school. Such absence is more frequent in the middle than in the manual working classes and partly owing to this, the average level of interest taken by parents in their children's education is actually higher in the families where the father was consistently away from home, than in those where he remained with the family. When allowances are made for the greater proportion of middle class fathers whose work demands that they are often away from home, there is evidence from the test scores that absence of the father is associated with poorer school work. At eight, after standardizing for social class, there is no difference between the average test scores of boys and girls whose fathers are consistently away from home and those whose fathers are never or seldom away. By eleven and even more by fifteen the former have fallen behind. The girls are more affected than the boys showing a deterioration of 1·7

* See Table 20.
† These figures refer only to the boys and girls of high ability.

[87]

points of test score between eight and fifteen compared with 1.3 for the boys. Owing to the small number of boys and girls whose fathers were consistently away and to the need to make allowances for both social class and ability when comparing the leaving dates and 'O' level results with the rest, it is not possible to reach any firm conclusion on the effects of fathers' absence on these two criteria of school performance.

It would be natural at this point to move on to a discussion of broken families. This however raises complex questions which can only be satisfactorily answered in the general setting of insecure family circumstances. This will be the subject of a later book; the impact of death of the father is however briefly discussed in the next chapter.

In 1961 the mothers were asked about their hopes and aspirations for their children's future employment. As would be expected, there are great differences between the choices made by parents from the different social classes; 56 per cent of the upper middle class parents hope that their sons will enter the professions—including accountancy, teaching, etc.—compared with only 5 per cent of those from the lower manual working class.

Although the actual proportion of upper middle class parents who hope that their sons will enter a profession is large, the small number of families of this type in the whole population means that only 14 per cent of the professional workers in the next generation will, if their parents wishes mean anything, be recruited from the upper middle class, which includes the majority of the parents who are themselves in the professions. If these expectations are fulfilled, it seems that the recruitment to the professions from the manual working class will be many times greater in the next generation than in the previous one—only 1 in 5 of the *fathers* in the professions had manual working class origins, whereas 1 in 2 of the new generation of professional workers should have them.

The parents' views of their children's jobs appear to be fairly realistic when they are looked at in relation to ability. The average ability of the boys who are expected to enter the professions is 60·8 at fifteen years; in contrast, those expected to enter manual occupations make low scores in all tests, 46·8. The former make higher scores in the attainment than in the non-verbal tests of ability, whereas those expected to enter manual work show the opposite pattern.

Parents in the different social classes have very different ambitions for their children even if on our tests their ability appears to be similar; for example 79 per cent of upper middle class boys of high ability are expected to enter the professions, compared with only 39 per cent of the lower manual working class boys of similar ability. The differences are even more pronounced at the border line level of ability. Here 48 per cent of the middle class parents expect their sons to enter the professions, but only 7 per cent of the lower manual working class.* The low expectations of the manual working class parents may reflect the real difficulties that many talented pupils have in attempting to enter the professions when they lack skilled advice and encouragement from their parents and schools.

The effects of the parents' own education is even more marked than the effects of social class. It is particularly those who themselves have been to the universities who expect their children to enter the professions and this is so at each level of ability. In fact, it seems that some parents with high educational attainments themselves have expectations for their sons that are unrealistic, for example 45 per cent of parents with better than secondary education who have sons of around average ability, 45–55 in the fifteen year tests, expect them to seek employment at a professional level. Here conflicts are to be expected between parental hopes and what the boys are actually capable of achieving.

To summarize, education widens the horizon for each generation and this in turn affects the level of attainment of the children, shaping their ambitions for the future. Parents who have themselves enjoyed a high standard of education see the necessity of education for the future employment of their children while others, who have failed to get the education they aimed at for themselves, try to ensure that the chances they have missed will be taken up by their children. It is sometimes assumed that the better educated move up the social ladder because they are the most able and that the schools and universities sift out the best endowed and give them opportunities to rise. This is how many would wish it to be. The vigour and quality of present day society depends on the efficiency with which the educa-

* See Table 21.

[89]

tional system sifts out the able pupils from all levels, and allows them to qualify for posts of responsibility. The evidence of this study shows how far short we are falling. While the way is, in theory, open for all those who have the ability, the influence of the family and the encouragement that the family can give are still important elements in the level of employment achieved by each individual.

Chapter Thirteen

Ill or Disabled Parents

A recent study (Rutter, 1966) of 922 children receiving treatment at a psychiatric clinic, showed an association between psychiatric disorder in children and illness of their parents. This association, though most marked with parental mental disorder, was also present for chronic physical illness, and the death of either parent. Boys in Rutter's study appeared to be affected more than girls by parental ill health and in general were more disturbed by their fathers' illnesses, whereas the girls were more disturbed by their mothers'. The total amount of illness in the family was however also important and when both parents were ill their children were particularly at risk.

If the illness of parents can precipitate severe mental illness in some children, it is reasonable to expect that it will lead to less profound but nevertheless detectable signs of disturbed behaviour in others. If so, these disturbances are likely to show themselves at school as well as elsewhere and in work as well as behaviour. For some, performance may actually improve as a result of efforts to compensate for problems at home, for others it may deteriorate. Apart from any direct influence of this sort on a pupil's general stability, concentration and attitude, a child whose father or mother is an invalid or confined indoors is likely to be kept away from school to help at home, and for this reason alone may fall behind other members of the class who are absent less frequently.

We have details of maternal ill health associated with and immediately following the 1946 births, but it was not until 15 years later that the mothers were asked again about their health; on this second occasion questions about the health of the father were also included.

They covered common complaints, such as asthma or rheumatism, chronic disabilities or physical handicaps, and a history of all in-patient admissions since 1946. These were recorded separately for each parent. In addition, details were collected about any illness that had kept the father off work for a long period. Lastly, the mothers were asked to summarize their own and their husbands' health on a five point scale, running from excellent to bad.

Many criticisms can be made of the reliability of this information. We rely heavily on the memories of women over a period of many years and are assuming that they will be able to recall not only their own illnesses but those of their husbands. Accordingly no attempt has been made to do more than group the fathers and mothers by their general health, into three broad categories; first, those whose health was said to be excellent or good, i.e. who had no complaints or chronic disabilities and spent less than one month in hospital during the preceeding 15 years; second, those who were said to be in excellent, good or average health but had some complaint or chronic disability or had spent more than a month in hospital; third, those said to be in poor or very poor health.

The older husbands are more likely to be picked out by their wives as in poor health than the younger; on the other hand, there is no increase with age in the illnesses reported by the mothers for themselves. Among the husbands there is a considerable increase in the time lost from work owing to illness, in passing from those described as healthy (only 1 per cent had ever lost more than 6 months at a stretch) to those in poor health (27 per cent); on the other hand there is a strong tendency for women who see themselves as in poor health to describe their husbands similarly; for example only 10 per cent of the women who had no complaints about their own health said that their husbands were in poor health, compared with 43 per cent of those who described their own health as bad or poor. The answers moreover appear to be influenced by personality. The mothers who, on the shortened version of the Maudsley Personality Inventory* chose a high proportion of statements associated with neurotic behaviour, are more likely to see themselves as being in poor health than those who rejected these statements.

* See Glossary.

[92]

Thus only 9 per cent of women in good health had high neurotic scores on the inventory compared with 26 per cent of those in poor health.

Finally, the reports of both the fathers' and the mothers' health are less favourable in the manual working than in the middle class. In each class however the mothers gave a less favourable account of their own than of their husbands' health—an observation that is not unexpected when it is rememberd that in all studies of general practice women are found to make many more calls on their family doctors than men.

When either the father or mother is in poor health school attendance falls off except for the middle class boys. This, although true for both boys and girls, is more marked for the latter. It appears that girls are kept away from school to help in the house, though this explanation which directly links domestic needs with time lost, is inadequate since the increase in absences occurs whether the illness is of the father or the mother. When there is little illness in the family, middle class girls lose considerably less time from school than manual working class girls; as illness increases however this difference narrows. For example in passing from families where the mothers' health is good to families where it is poor, there is a four-fold rise in the proportion of middle class girls with many absences, compared with a two-fold rise for manual working class girls.

Lack of interest and encouragement at home does not explain the high rate of absence among children whose parents are ill since our assessments of interest alter little with the state of health of the family, nor do the children themselves show appreciably less interest in their work if their parents are ill; they are nearly as likely as the rest to be regarded by their teachers as good or hard workers and this is so in each social class and for both the boys and the girls.

The main handicap of these pupils, so far as we can see, lies in their intermittent attendance at school. As judged by the tests given at fifteen, the health of the parents has some influence on the attainment and ability of their sons and daughters but this perhaps is less than might be expected. Those whose parents are in poor health make rather lower scores in all tests, non-verbal as much as attainment, though we would have expected that their mathematics

[93]

and reading scores would be more depressed because they lost a greater than average amount of time from school.

A child of the same sex as the parent who is ill is no more, or less, likely to be affected than one of the opposite sex. Accordingly, parental illness has been summarized by dividing the families into three groups putting those in which both parents are in excellent or good health at one extreme, and those in which one or both are in poor health at the other.

In the General Certificate of Education examination there is no consistent evidence that the parents' health influences the level of certificate obtained or indeed the chances of obtaining any certificate at all, once ability is taken into account. The only one of our criteria of achievement that is in any way markedly linked to parents' health is the age of leaving school; from both selective and secondary modern schools, pupils with ill parents leave early, particularly in the manual working classes.* This suggests that the effect of parental ill health will become increasingly evident for the more able pupils in the later years at school, when the proportion who stay on and therefore have a chance to take 'A' levels and enter the university will be higher among those with healthy mothers and fathers.

The group of parents in poor health includes fathers and mothers with a whole variety of illnesses ranging from the crippling to those having relatively little effect on ordinary activities, work or the daily routine of the family. The effects of parental ill health on school attainment are however marked in two special groups, when the father is unemployed owing to illness and when he has died.

Out of 99 fathers who were unemployed at the time of the 1961 inquiry, illness prevented 85 from working; 13 others were un-employed for various other reasons and 1 was unable to work because as a widower he had been forced to do the family house-keeping. The majority of the 85 fathers off work owing to illness had been in poor health for more than a year; only 12 had illnesses of a shorter duration. Many of these long term illnesses were serious physical conditions, such as osteomyelitis, cerebral haemorrhage, gangrene with amputation of both legs or progressive muscular dystrophy. Only 5 are known to have been kept away from work for purely psychiatric reasons, though this is perhaps an under-

* See Table 22.

[94]

estimate. There may have been a disproportionate amount of non-co-operation in those families in which there were psychiatric disturbances, and the separation and divorce rate may be unduly high in this group. In some instances a psychiatric element may be inferred, for example a father concussed in an accident was still away from work several years later. Unfortunately our information is insufficient to discriminate between physical illnesses with and without psychiatric overtones.

While unemployment through illness is found in each social class, it is in excess in the lower manual working class; 79 per cent of the reported instances of unemployment were in this class, nearly twice as many as would be expected. The families of the ill and unemployed are also large; 58 per cent have four or more children compared with 33 per cent in the whole sample.

In view of the high representation of large families from the manual working classes, one would expect the test performance and school progress of those with unemployed fathers to be relatively low, and this is so. In the tests at each age, the children whose fathers were unemployed through illness make scores that are on the average approximately 6 points below the average for the whole sample and 1·7 points below the expected average when allowances are made for their social class, size of family, standards of care and housing conditions.* Thus taking account of their family circumstances has greatly reduced, though not fully explained, their relatively poorer test performance. It should be noted however that they have similarly low scores in both intelligence and attainment. There is moreover no close association between the date of onset of the illness leading to unemployment and a deterioration in test score.

One group of illnesses leading to unemployment is associated with relatively high test scores. The 16 children whose fathers had coronary heart disease, strokes, or other cardiovascular diseases make scores in the fifteen year tests that are 5·9 points above those expected after allowing for their social class, family size, housing and maternal care. The boys and girls with fathers unemployed owing to other illnesses were 3·8 points below the expected average score and they were similarly handicapped whether their fathers were off work for chronic infections, disability following accidents, illnesses with a

* See Table 23.

[95]

psychosomatic element, or other illnesses such as disseminated sclerosis or leukaemia.

In the selective schools, relatively few of the children of the ill and unemployed fathers remain to start the 1962/3 session, 40 per cent as compared with 71 per cent in the rest of the population. At secondary modern schools also, only 16 per cent stayed on after fifteen years compared with an expected 35 per cent. Here then is a relatively small group of families in which serious and incapacitating illness of the father, followed in many instances by financial hardship, is associated with poor progress of the children at school and early leaving.

The number of boys and girls in the Educational Sample who lost their fathers through death is 165; 52 of these deaths occurred during the first 6 years of the Survey.* The families in which the father died were materially considerably worse off than the rest, a higher proportion than expected being lower manual working class. Standards of maternal care, as assessed by the health visitors, were low, housing conditions were poor not only owing to the large size of the families, but also to the fact that many were sharing their homes or rooms with relatives. One hundred and thirty-three of these deaths (32 early, i.e. in the first 6 years, and 101 later), were not, as far as we know, related to long periods of illness.

At fifteen years of age, the aggregate test scores are not in any way depressed for those whose fathers died suddenly, whether this was by six years or later. The average aggregate scores of those whose fathers died after a long illness are however considerably and significantly depressed at fifteen and this is so even after allowances have been made for family size, standards of maternal care, housing and social class.† The greatest handicap is when the father died after a long period of illness while the child was at school. The average scores of these boys and girls are 5·5 points below those expected after allowing for their family circumstances. It must however be emphasized that although this difference is statistically significant it is based on 12 children and that only 32 fathers died after long illnesses during the whole fifteen year period. For these families all the test scores are depressed, the non-verbal as much as the verbal

* Only 78 boys and girls in the Educational Sample lost their mothers.
† See Table 24.

[96]

and attainment. Only three of the children who had lost their fathers through death after a long illness went to selective secondary schools. Among the 26 secondary modern school pupils, only two remained to complete the 1961/2 session.

The attainment of the children who lose their fathers by sudden death, early or late, is no lower than would be expected. They are as likely to reach the selective schools and as likely to stay at school as those with fathers who were still alive and living with the family. Thus although the sudden death of a parent may involve considerable deterioration in the living conditions of the family, it has relatively little effect on a child's school progress. Those that are handicapped are the children whose fathers have experienced long periods of illness before death and the more recent this experience the more affected they are. Prolonged strain, worry and adjustments in family routine to care for an ill parent, or the stresses thrown on the family by a long period of unemployment of the father, take their toll of a child's school attainment. It seems probable that family insecurity associated with prolonged illness, rather than the shock of the father's death, is the factor leading to poor educational performance.

Chapter Fourteen

Aspirations, Interests and Attitudes to Work

Job Aspirations

The parents' views on the type of work that they hoped their children would eventually enter were described in Chapter XII. The Survey members, when they were fifteen years, were asked about their own job plans or aspirations. When the job choices and hopes are grouped into three broad categories, professional work, other non-manual jobs and manual work, there is close agreement between the choices of the children and the hopes of their parents; only 13 per cent of the boys and 9 per cent of the girls wished to take up work in a different group from that hoped for by their parents. Disagreement would have been higher of course if a finer grouping of occupations had been used, but in the present context it is a broad description that is relevant. Eight per cent of the parents would like their sons to take jobs at a higher level than those selected by the sons themselves, while 5 per cent would wish them to take jobs at a lower level. In these conflicting instances, the parents appear on the whole to be making a fair assessment of their sons' abilities—for example, the average test scores of boys who wish to go into clerical work but whose parents would have liked them to enter a profession, are closer to the average for all boys wishing to enter the professions, than they are to those of all boys aiming for clerical work. Conversely, the average scores of the boys who say they want to go into clerical occupations but whose parents have stipulated manual work are close to those of boys hoping for manual work. Among the girls the discrepancies are similar. Four per cent of the parents have aspirations that are lower and 5 per cent aspirations that are higher; as with the boys they give a fair assessment of their daughters' ability.

Judged by average test performance, the fifteen year old job choices of members of the National Survey were not unrealistic. Those who named a profession are mainly pupils of high ability and the test scores of this aspiring group are similar in each social class—this does not mean however that at any given level of ability the chance of entering a profession is independent of the social background of the family. Indeed as will be shown later, this is far from being so.

The few girls who wish to go into manual work are of very low ability, scoring an average of 41 in the fifteen year tests, compared with 47 for the boys with similar intentions; this underlines the unskilled nature of the manual employment available for women—mainly repetitive work in light industry.

Other studies have shown that the job hopes and aspirations of adolescents are to a large extent moulded by the people they meet and the kind of employment open to them in the areas where they live. Horizons are limited by lack of knowledge, and job choices are frequently made within a frame of reference that is only wide enough to include those types of employment pursued by members of their families, relatives or friends in the neighbourhood. In this study it is clear that the job hopes of these boys and girls are often more closely related to their home circumstances than to their potential ability.

Approximately half of the upper middle class boys and girls hoped to enter the professions compared with only 5 per cent of the lower manual working class. A major part of this large discrepancy is of course explained by differences in ability but even after allowances have been made for this, considerable social class differences in aspirations remain; for example 48 per cent of the boys in the borderline group for admission to grammar school from the upper middle class said that they hoped to enter a profession compared with 7 per cent from the lower manual working class—indeed amongst the latter as high a proportion as 56 per cent expected to take up manual work, compared with only 5 per cent of those from the upper middle class.* At the other end of the ability scale, there are relatively small differences in the hopes of pupils from different social classes. A similar proportion of boys of less than average ability and attainment at fifteen years from each social class intend to enter manual work.

* See Table 25.

[99]

The main social difference for this level lies in the higher proportion of upper middle class boys who hope to be self-employed. In the other social classes low grade clerical work is the alternative to manual work.

Similar social class differences are found for the girls except that, at the lower levels of ability, the upper middle class girls are more likely than the rest to have plans to enter professions such as nursing.

When the children are grouped by their parents' education rather than by their social class, these differences are increased—in the border line group 60 per cent of the boys and girls whose parents had been only to elementary schools expect to enter manual work, compared with none of the children whose parents had more than secondary education.

These comparisons leave us in no doubt that there is a large group of young men and women who, though potentially capable of entering one of the professions, choose manual work. The reason for this lies partly perhaps in the fact that they are unable to see themselves as following a way of life that is radically different from that of their parents and the rest of their family and friends. If their expectations are fulfilled the new generation of manual workers will contain many of high ability; 18 per cent will, it seems, be in the top third of measured ability and 5 per cent in the top sixth. Whether or not this is to be deplored depends on the reader's point of view. On the one hand there will be no lack of able men to negotiate with their employers and provide executive officers for trades unions; on the other, the professions and non-manual occupations will be relatively the worse off. But whether one regrets this or not, the fact remains that more than half of the boys of high ability from manual working class homes are unlikely to move out of the social class into which they were born.

The boys who hope to enter the professions show a steady improvement in test performance during their years at school. The difference between their average aggregate scores and those of boys hoping to enter manual work is 12·8 points at eight years rising to 14·2 at fifteen. For the girls, the parallel figures are 17·6 at eight and 19·2 seven years later. Those aiming at the professions, in addition to improving their test scores, are also over-achievers in the sense that their verbal and attainment test scores are higher than their non-

[100]

verbal intelligence. The boys in particular have high mathematics scores.

At each level of ability the boys and girls who say that they are aiming at a professional training, as would be expected if they were making realistic choices, get more and better General Certificates than those whose plans are for either manual or non-manual work. These differences are dramatic; for example at ability 50–59, 34 per cent of the boys who hope for professional careers get good 'O' level certificates, compared with 8 per cent of those aiming for other non-manual work and 6 per cent of those who hope for manual work. Similar differences are found for the girls.

The age of leaving school, as would be expected, is also closely related to job aspirations. In the selective schools, 91 per cent of the boys who said at fifteen that they hoped to enter a profession are still at school at the beginning of the 1962/3 session, compared with only 56 per cent of those aiming for other non-manual work and 51 per cent of those aiming for manual. Among the secondary modern school pupils, the differences are even larger; only 9 per cent of those hoping for manual work finished the session 1961/2, compared with 88 per cent of those who hoped for some sort of professional job, even at a relatively low level.

Leisure Interests

The home background of a pupil, by widening or limiting his contacts, shapes a major part of his plans for the future and, in a broader context, also has a considerable influence on what he does in his spare time—his hobbies and club membership. The mothers were asked, when the Survey members were eleven years old, about their sons' and daughters' club membership, main hobbies and interests; at thirteen and fifteen, the boys and girls themselves were asked similar questions. The information collected on these three occasions has been used to group the boys and girls by their out of school activities. A simple division into those who never joined a club and the rest, yields some interesting associations, both social and educational. It is rare for the pupils never to have joined a club, including religious organizations, Scouts and Guides. Only 16 per cent of the boys and 15 per cent of the girls never joined. In the lower manual working class however the figure rises to 21 per cent for the boys and

[101]

19 per cent for the girls. The average test scores of non-members are low as would be expected from the relatively high proportion of manual working class pupils among them. Within each social class however there is a relatively constant gap of roughly 4 points of aggregate test score between those who never joined a club and those who are members at fifteen. Intermediate are those pupils who joined clubs in the early school years but were not members at fifteen. Those who had never joined have particularly low scores in mathematics and in general their attainment and verbal ability scores are lower than their non-verbal intelligence test scores—this is so in each social class and at each age.

Even taking account of their lower ability, the pupils who are not club members do relatively poorly both in the 11+ selection examinations and the General Certificate of Education. They also leave school, particularly secondary modern school, earlier than the club members. It seems therefore that by the simple criterion of club membership, it is possible to pick out pupils who are making good or poor progress at school.

The boys and girls have also been divided into three groups, according to their hobbies at eleven, thirteen and fifteen years. The first comprises all those who reported academic interests or hobbies at any age (nature study, writing to foreign pen-friends, stamp collecting, etc.) whatever other hobbies they had; the second comprises those with no academic interest, but with artistic and practical hobbies (those who drew, played an instrument, acted, or took an interest in carpentry, needlework or dressmaking); the third comprises those interested only in sport.

No boys or girls were without hobbies. Academic hobbies are more often reported in the middle classes—36 per cent of the upper middle class boys had at least one academic hobby, but only 16 per cent of the lower manual working class. Interest in sport alone is recorded however for only 28 per cent of the upper middle class boys compared with 52 per cent of the lower manual working class. For the girls, similar social class differences are found for academic hobbies, but there is no suggestion that manual working class girls are interested in sport to the exclusion of other pastimes.

The boys and girls who have academic hobbies have higher test scores than the rest. There is little difference between the boys who are mainly interested in arts and the boys who are mainly interested in sport, but the girls who gave sport as their only interest have higher test scores than those who gave art, perhaps because the latter include those solely interested in dressmaking or some other domestic occupation. At each age, the boys and the girls with academic hobbies are approximately 5 points of test score above the rest, their advantage lies more in attainment than in non-verbal tests.

There are more pupils with academic interests at selective schools and, at all types of school, those with academic interests are more likely to stay on. In the General Certificate examination, however, once intelligence and attainment have been allowed for, they have no advantage.

Spare time interests therefore have some predictive value for a pupil's standard of work and this is so whether hobbies or club membership is used as the criterion.

Attitude to Work

When these boys and girls were at primary school, the teachers were asked to rate their attitude to work. These ratings were crude, being based on the single question 'Is the child in general a very hard worker, a hard worker, an average worker, a poor worker or lazy?' Very few teachers were prepared to say that a pupil was lazy, and there was a general reluctance to give unfavourable estimates— for instance 17 per cent were said to work less hard than average, compared with 38 per cent who worked harder. In spite of this, the attainment of children in primary schools and the level of interest taken by their parents were both closely related to the teachers' ratings—on the whole the pupils with highly interested parents worked hard and did well in the tests and in the 11+ examinations, whereas those with parents who took little interest and gave them little encouragement were often poor workers and lazy, and did poorly in both tests and examinations.

The secondary school teachers were asked in much more detail about the attitude and behaviour of their pupils. The questions covered three main areas. First, how hard they worked, their powers of concentration and neatness of work; second, how restless they were in class, whether they daydreamed, how they reacted to

[103]

discipline, whether they were obedient, and whether they cribbed or lied to evade trouble; third, their behaviour outside the classroom. Only the first two of these areas are discussed here; out of class behaviour is discussed in the next chapter.

The teachers made all these assessments twice, the first when the Survey members were thirteen years old and the second two years later. This means that for each pupil reports are available from two different teachers. These have been combined to give overall assessments of 'attitude to work' and 'class behaviour'; each assessment is used to divide the pupils into three groups, those whose attitude to work was 'good', 'fair' or 'poor', and those who were 'well behaved', 'moderately well behaved' or 'troublesome'.

When the assessments of attitude to work at the primary school are compared with the more detailed assessments made in the secondary school, agreement between the two is relatively good: the pupils who are reported as hard working early in their school careers are for the most part hard working later on. This association is as marked for the middle class boys and girls as for those from the manual working class. The attitude to work of some pupils however appears to have changed considerably; 17 per cent of the poor or lazy workers in the primary schools are reported as hard working in the secondary. On the other hand, 7 per cent of those who were said to be hard working in the primary school are poorly assessed in the secondary. The amount of support that the parents give their children with their school work and the level of interest they show in their academic progress is closely related to these changes. The children of parents who take little interest are four times as likely to deteriorate in their attitude to work between the primary and secondary stage, as those whose parents take a high level of interest. Conversely pupils who are fortunate enough to have highly interested parents are twice as likely to improve.

In the secondary schools, as well as in the primary, the relation between the pupils' attitude to work and parental support and encouragement is close, although by no means complete. There are many pupils, from all types of family, who work hard even though their parents show little interest, and similarly there are many who are idle, though their parents are anxious that they should succeed. The association between high interest and hard work, on the one

[104]

hand, and low interest and poor work, on the other, is more marked for pupils from manual working than from middle class families.

A pupil's behaviour in the class-room is of course also associated with attitude to work: those who work hard tend to be those who give least trouble, whereas those who are reported as poor workers are the most troublesome, and moreover the parents of these children take relatively little interest in their studies. The reverse pattern of poor workers who are well behaved is too rare for comment.

The selective school pupils were assessed more favourably for their attitudes to work and class behaviour than those at the secondary modern schools; in other words, the pupils at selective schools are seen as harder working and as giving less trouble to those who teach them than pupils at non-selective schools. This is so for both boys and girls, though in each type of school the behaviour of the girls is more favourably assessed than the behaviour of the boys.

As the teachers appear to be picking out pupils with similar characteristics whether they are reporting on their attitude to work or their class behaviour, these two assessments were combined to produce a composite rating which separates out approximately 25 per cent of the best behaved and hardest working pupils, and 25 per cent of the worst behaved and least studious, from an intermediate group of approximately 50 per cent.

The well behaved and hard working pupils are the most likely to say that they hope to enter the professions, they are the most likely to have academic hobbies, and more of them are club members at fifteen.

There is a progressive divergence in ability among the three groups during their school careers. The hard working and well behaved improve their position relative to those who are poor workers and troublesome. Thus at eight years of age there is a 7·6 points difference for the boys which increases to 11·3 points seven years later. A similar, though rather smaller, divergence is found for the girls.

In each social class the boys and girls who are hard working and well behaved make on the average the highest scores in each test, and those who are poor workers or troublesome make the lowest, the differences being rather greater in the attainment and verbal

[105]

tests than in the non-verbal. For the boys the hard working and well behaved have their greatest advantage in mathematics, whereas for the girls similar differences hold for the two attainment and the verbal intelligence tests. When the boys are grouped by social class as well as by their attitude to work and behaviour in school, the hard working and well behaved middle class boys are outstanding in mathematics, while the lower manual working class boys are no more at an advantage in mathematics than in reading or verbal intelligence.

The results of the General Certificate of Education also show large differences between these groups even after the ability of the boys and girls has been taken into account. Thus for boys of high ability 73 per cent of the hard working and well behaved gained good certificates compared with only 35 per cent of the troublesome and poor workers.

In the selective schools the boys and girls who are troublesome and poor workers leave early. For example 47 per cent of these girls leave school before the start of the session 1962/3 compared with only 24 per cent of the hard working and well behaved. Differences in the secondary modern schools are even greater; 94 per cent of the girls who are poor workers and troublesome leave before the end of the session 1961/2 compared with only 66 per cent of the hard workers and well behaved.

The teachers' comments on behaviour in class and attitude to work pick out groups of pupils who, during their time at school, show a relative improvement or deterioration in their measured attainment, and who differ greatly in their 'O' level results and age of leaving. We have already mentioned that the teachers were also asked to assess the behaviour of the boys and girls out of class. These additional ratings are discussed in the next chapter.

Chapter Fifteen

Emotional Adjustment and School Progress*

The first tests of intelligence, pioneered in Paris by Simon and Binet at the beginning of this century, were developed to separate out a special group of pupils, namely those who were failing at school, not because of lack of ability, but because of various character and personality defects (Binet and Simon, 1916). A series of graduated questions, largely unrelated to school work, was used to construct a scale which would identify those who had the ability to learn but had not used it, from those who genuinely did not have the capacity. The former were to be given special help at school, so that their academic standard might improve. At that time, some 60 years ago, the link between behaviour difficulties and backwardness was recognized, although it was thought that these barriers to school learning applied to school subjects only, as opposed to intellectual exercises with no close relation to formal lessons; the more so because the latter were given in a standardized form that required no prolonged effort of concentration.

In *The Home and the School* it was reported that eleven year olds who bit their nails, wet their beds, had recurrent nightmares or bouts of unexplained abdominal pain, or recurrent vomiting, were educationally handicapped in many ways. They made low scores in all tests, including non-verbal intelligence, and at each level of measured ability gained fewer grammar school places than those who did not have these habits or symptoms. Their teachers tended to describe them as poor workers, lacking in concentration and

* Many technical questions are raised but left unanswered in this chapter. They will be discussed in a later publication on the relation between anxiety-provoking events within the family and subsequent behaviour.

[107]

having difficulties in their relations with their class-mates. It was moreover not just the small group of pupils with many symptoms who were handicapped in these ways, for there was a fall in average ability and attainment with each increase above one in the number of symptoms reported, whichever symptom it was.

During the secondary school years, a special effort was made to collect information, from a variety of additional sources, relevant to the emotional adjustment and behaviour of the pupils in this study. We were not primarily interested in identifying the severely disturbed or those under treatment, since much has been written about the educational handicaps of this extreme group, whereas little is known about the problems of those with minor peculiarities of behaviour.

There are few children who do not have any habits or symptoms at all, but there is no means of deciding how many or what combinations of these need to be present before a child can be identified as requring special or extra help, whether this be medical, psychological or educational.

Information on the general behaviour of the Survey pupils comes from three main sources: (a) the teachers' assessments of behaviour out of class, (b) the mothers' reports of symptoms that are generally considered to be associated with disturbed behaviour, (c) a self-rating inventory completed by the boys and girls when they were thirteen years old. By using these three descriptions of the pupils, it was hoped to obtain information on various dimensions of behaviour that might be affecting attainment and school progress in different ways.

(a) *The Teachers' Ratings*

When the children were ten years old, their teachers were asked to comment on discipline and difficulties with school-mates. In addition to these questions asked for all pupils, there was an open question asking for any comments the teachers wished to make; this elicited a number of references to behaviour, the majority of which mentioned shyness, nervousness, withdrawal or aggression. This open question was not specifically directed at abnormalities of behaviour, and the type of answer will have depended on the special interests of the teacher as well as on the characteristics of the child. It has been of value however in showing that the teachers are prepared to differentiate the withdrawn or nervous pupil from the troublesome or aggressive.

When the pupils were thirteen and again when they were fifteen, the teachers were asked to rate them as 'above average', 'average' or 'below average' on a large number of items of behaviour and personal characteristics, including nervousness, attention seeking, dare devilry, competitiveness, aggressiveness, ability to make friends, energy, anxiousness and attitudes towards criticism and punishment. After making these ratings, the teachers were asked to make over-all assessments of sensitiveness, shyness and aggressiveness for each pupil. Although this list of assessments seems formidable the teachers' task was relatively light for they were seldom asked to rate more than one pupil in a class.

The teachers' behaviour ratings at both thirteen and fifteen years were combined and used to define five groups of pupils—three with high ratings for either nervousness or aggressiveness or both (these three groups together comprised 31 per cent of the sample): a fourth with medium ratings (41 per cent of the sample) and a fifth with low ratings (28 per cent). The comparatively large size of these groups is emphasized: none comprises solely those who were seriously disturbed. Indeed the teachers' comments have been used to group the boys and girls by their possession of certain frequently recognized traits, rather than to identify a small group of abnormal pupils.

There is very little difference in the proportion of adverse ratings made by teachers in selective and secondary modern schools. This is in striking contrast to the class attitude ratings which pick out the secondary modern pupils as far more troublesome in class than the selective school pupils. There is also surprisingly little social class difference in the behaviour ratings within each type of school, though rather more of the manual working than of the middle class boys at secondary modern schools are picked out as aggressive. In view of the smallness of the differences in the ratings given to pupils at selective and secondary modern schools, all types of school are considered together in this chapter.

In order to find out whether the teachers, in making these ratings, were identifying pupils with real behaviour problems rather than merely picking out those who were making little progress at

[109]

school, similar assessments were obtained from teachers for 200 thirteen year olds not enrolled in the National Survey, who were attending Child Guidance Clinics, and had been clinically assessed by a psychiatrist as either nervous or aggressive. Taking these two assessed groups of Child Guidance attenders and a third matched group of similar size drawn from the National Survey thirteen year olds with no history of behaviour problems, it was found that the teachers' ratings classified 7 out of 10 correctly as nervous, aggressive or 'normal' (Mulligan, 1964).

That the teachers' behaviour ratings in this special validation study put 70 per cent of the pupils into their correct clinical groupings is not wholly convincing evidence of the value of these assessments, for we do not know how many of the teachers were aware that their pupils were undergoing treatment. Further supporting evidence of the usefulness of the ratings comes however from several sources within the National Survey. A relatively high proportion of boys and girls with high ratings had at some time attended clinics or hospitals for the treatment of behaviour problems; it is not possible however to say whether the teachers knew of the treatment given. Similar reservations have to be made when evaluating the fact that police cautions and court sentences were most frequent, 25 per cent, among the boys with high aggressive ratings, and least frequent, 8 per cent, among those with high nervous ratings.

The best supporting evidence of the validity of the teachers' behaviour ratings comes from the comparison with independent reports from the mothers, who were asked at earlier home visits and medical examinations about their children's general behaviour. The pupils, who by their secondary school teachers' ratings were classed as aggressive, or mixed nervous and aggressive, were the most likely to be reported earlier by their mothers as having committed aggressive or anti-social acts, and similarly those reported by their teachers as nervous, or mixed nervous and aggressive, were more likely to have nervous behaviour reported earlier by their mothers. A consistent picture also emerges when the comments of the primary school teachers, who were not concerned with the aggressive and nervous ratings as such, are compared with the secondary school teachers' ratings.

The relation between the teachers' behaviour ratings and the neurotic items of the self-rating inventory, completed at thirteen, is described later. There is however another scale in the self-rating inventory that is relevant to the validity of the teachers' ratings of nervousness and aggressiveness, namely the extraversion-introversion scale. As might perhaps be expected, the nervous pupils are more introverted than extraverted, and the aggressive are more extraverted than introverted, whereas the mixed nervous and aggressive have a distribution of responses on this scale that is almost the same as for those pupils with low ratings for both nervousness and aggression.

A further interesting association is that the pupils with high aggressive ratings had a large number of accidents treated by the family doctor or in hospital in the first eleven years of their lives, while those with high nervous ratings had relatively few. There is no possibility here that the teachers can have known of the number of accidents these pupils had, particularly as many of these were in early life.

The pupils with high ratings for nervousness or aggression, or both of these, make low scores in all the fifteen year tests, their average being 47·3 compared with 50·1 for those with medium ratings, and 52·0 for those with low. The nervous pupils do no better in the non-verbal than in the attainment tests, but the aggressive and mixed nervous and aggressive pupils tended to make rather higher scores in the non-verbal test than in the others, and so to some extent may be regarded as under-achievers.

There is no evidence from the earlier tests at eight and eleven that either the nervous or aggressive pupils have deteriorated in measured ability and attainment during their years at school. It seems that, in their assessments of the out of class behaviour of pupils, the secondary school teachers are picking out those who at every stage of their school careers have a relatively low level of performance in the tests. This is in striking contrast to the pupils picked out by the same teachers as having a poor attitude to work or being troublesome in class. These pupils show a deterioration in attainment between eight and fifteen which suggests increasing lack of interest rather than a lack of ability.

The work habits of the nervous and aggressive pupils are very different. Those picked out as nervous are on the average hard workers and well behaved in class; they are seldom truant though

[111]

they have more absences than expected. In contrast, those with high aggressive ratings or mixed aggressive and nervous ratings are more often troublesome in the class-room and outside, neglect their studies and are likely to be truant. Similar differences between these groups are found in the primary schools, i.e. before the ratings were made, as well as later.

In their reports on these pupils' behaviour the teachers are giving high ratings to two different types of child; the nervous who work hard, give no trouble in class and yet do badly in their tests and in their work, and the aggressive or mixed nervous and aggressive, many of whom do not take their studies seriously, and are troublesome at school. The nervous pupils in the non-verbal tests make as low scores as the aggressive or mixed, but in the tests of attainment their performance is slightly though not significantly better. What is surprising, considering their seriousness and industry at school, is that they neither make significantly higher scores in attainment than in non-verbal tests nor improve their relative position in the attainment tests between eight and fifteen years.

(b) *Symptoms*

The symptoms that were asked about at fifteen were stammering, nail biting, unexplained vomiting and abdominal pain, bedwetting, thumb sucking, and other habits—these when added together give a score running from nought to eight. Similar scores are available at six and eleven years.* The fifteen year score differs from the earlier ones in that information on nail biting, thumb sucking, stammering and other symptoms was obtained from the teachers and not the mothers. Thus the symptom counts at fifteen are not wholly independent of the teachers as were those at six and eleven, and it might be suggested that there would be a tendency for the pupils who were picked out by the teachers as aggressive or nervous to be also identified as having symptoms of various sorts. Rather more of the nervous and aggressive have many symptoms at fifteen but they also are more likely to have many symptoms at eleven, though at this age the teachers made no contribution.

As the number of symptoms increases, attitudes to school deterior-

* Nail biting is counted twice if reported by both mother and doctor at six and eleven, or both teacher and doctor at fifteen.

[112]

ate; those with symptoms are more likely to lose time from school, to have episodes of truancy, to be less well behaved in class and to be reported as poor workers. Test performance also deteriorates and even one symptom is associated with a depression of test scores. There is also a suggestion that the gap between the test performance of those with many and those with no symptoms at fifteen has progressively widened since eight. All types of test are similarly affected and there is no evidence that the pupils with two or more symptoms are under-achieving.

So far only fifteen year symptoms have been considered. The earlier counts show, though to a lesser extent than the fifteen year symptom counts, a decrease in average score as the number of symptoms increases. In other words the association between symptoms and measured ability increases as the pupils grow older. At eight, there is a gap of 1·4 points of test score between those who had two or more symptoms at six years and those with none; at eleven years, a gap of 2·2 and at fifteen of 4·1. This is perhaps not unexpected, because with increasing age the number of boys and girls with many reported symptoms decreases and those that have persistent symptoms or acquire them at a later age, are likely to be a more highly selected abnormal group.

(c) *The Self-rating Inventory*

The last of the three behaviour assessments was obtained from a self-rating inventory completed by the pupils when they were thirteen years old (Mulligan, 1964). It consisted of 15 statements describing attitudes and actions that are characteristic of neurotic children, 15 relating to introversion and extraversion. The boys and girls were asked to read each statement and say whether or not it described their own feelings or actions correctly, and scales of neuroticism and of introversion-extraversion were obtained from their answers. These scales should be free from any bias inherent in the teachers' assessments of work habits or behaviour though, as the teachers saw the completed inventories, the more sophisticated pupils might perhaps have rated themselves either to please or irritate.

We are only concerned in the following discussion with the neurotic section of this inventory, as it is here that the relation with attainment and school progress is most evident. The 15 neurotic statements

[113]

referred to gullibility, make believe, tiredness, sadness, fear of thunder and items which in general reflect anxiety and worry. When set against information gathered from other sources, it seems that the pupils' answers give a useful indication of their characteristics and personality. Those with scores in the top third of the neurotic scale were more often picked out by their teachers as being either aggressive or both aggressive and nervous, than the rest of the pupils; there is a high proportion of delinquents among them. Pupils with high neurotic scores are also more likely to bite their nails, wet their beds and show other symptoms of this type.

The average test scores of the pupils in the top third of the neuroticism scale are lower than those of the rest, and they do slightly less well in the attainment tests than in the non-verbal tests. Between the ages of eight and fifteen there is little change in the differences between the average scores of the neurotic and the non-neurotic groups. Their school records show high absence rates from secondary school, a relatively high proportion of truancy and many adverse comments from their teachers, both primary and secondary, on their habits of work and behaviour.

Summarizing the Assessments

So far we have considered only the test results of the boys and girls picked out as being nervous or aggressive, as having many symptoms or as choosing many neurotic items. We have seen that in all these groups test scores are depressed at each age, but not substantially more so at the later age of fifteen years than at eleven or eight. We have also seen that apart from the very nervous pupils who tend to be hard working and well behaved in class, those who are anxious, have many symptoms, or are aggressive are more likely to be rated by their teachers as poor workers and troublesome than the rest.

As these three assessments of behaviour seem to pick out pupils who, by and large, have similar educational difficulties, the next step is to combine the teachers' assessments with the reported symptoms and the self-rating neuroticism scores.

When test performance is related to both symptom counts and teachers' ratings, there is a fall in average score as symptoms increase, which occurs at each level of the teachers' ratings. These two assessments have been used to give three groups, one (29 per cent of the sample) has both low teacher ratings and low symptom scores, the second (24 per cent) has both high ratings and many symptoms, and the third (47 per cent) is intermediate. These three groups were further sub-divided by their scores on the self-rating inventory to provide six groups.

At each of the three levels of teachers' behaviour ratings and reported symptoms the pupils who chose a large number of neurotic statements made lower scores than those who chose few. The range of average test performance at fifteen now varies from 45·2 for those who have high ratings, high neuroticism scores and many symptoms, to 53·3 for those who have low ratings, low neuroticism scores and few symptoms—a difference of 8·1 test points. At eight years of age the difference was smaller, 5·9 points, but by eleven had increased to 7·0.* It is only the extreme groups whose performances show relative change between 8 and 15 years; the position of the inter-mediate groups remains relatively unchanged.

When intelligence and attainment test scores at fifteen are com-pared, it is only the small group who are picked out unfavourably by all three assessments that turn out to be under-achieving, their average scores for verbal tests, mathematics and reading being below their scores in the non-verbal tests. It is these boys and girls who provide a serious educational challenge both because their performance has deteriorated during their years at school, and because their attainment is below that to be expected from their non-verbal intelligence test scores. These are the pupils who leave school the earliest and present many educational and social problems including a relatively high risk of delinquency. Twenty-three per cent of the boys in this group have been cautioned or sentenced in the courts compared with 4 per cent of boys with consistently low ratings. Rather unexpectedly the 'O' level results bear only a small and inconsistent relation to the assessments of behaviour, once ability has been taken into account.†

The conclusion to be drawn from this study of the relation between behaviour and school performance is that it is not only the grossly disturbed children that are affected, there is a continuous gradient

* See Table 26.
† See Table 27.

in performance running from those who have few adverse teachers' comments, no symptoms reported by the mothers, and low neuroticism scores to those who are picked out by all three measures. The more adverse items reported the lower is the performance in school.

It is only in the most extreme group that there is evidence of a relative deterioration in performance during the years at school. For the majority with some or many symptoms, or signs, of disturbed behaviour test performance is equally poor at each age. This suggests that the basis of their educational difficulties lies in the pre-school years.

Chapter Sixteen

Delinquent Boys at School

The delinquents described in this chapter are the boys who, between the ages of eight and seventeen, were either cautioned by the police or sentenced by the courts: those acquitted, or those whose delinquent behaviour was not discovered or not reported are not included. There were 288 delinquent boys and 35 delinquent girls. These figures, when adjusted for the original sampling of the National Survey,* give delinquency rates of 15 and 2 per cent for the boys and girls respectively. Both rates are just below those expected from official statistics, probably owing to the fact that illegitimate children born during the survey week and immigrants to Great Britain since 1946 have been left out. As so few girls were delinquent, this chapter is concerned only with the boys.

The high proportion of middle class families in the sample means that relatively few boys got into trouble with the police. That there were only 288 delinquents makes it difficult to give a satisfactory account of either the age at which these offences were committed or the type of offence which varies from the apparently trivial, such as trespassing on railway property or riding bicycles without lights, to the apparently serious, such as robbery with violence. The common link is simply being discovered, referred to the police and either cautioned or sentenced.

Once a boy has been before the courts, it is difficult to make an objective analysis of the predisposing causes, and it is also hard to avoid making special efforts to uncover relationships in his earlier upbringing which fit current theories about young offenders. What is needed, though rarely available, is information that has been

* Only one out of every four manual workers' children was followed up.

[117]

collected year by year for a complete population of boys, whether delinquent or not. In the present study we are able to look back at the homes, early histories and educational progress of boys before, as well as after, they come before the courts.

It is recognized that many delinquents are poor scholars and appear to their teachers as bored, inattentive and badly behaved in class. Many also have a history of truancy. It is however not clear whether the delinquents are backward because they lack ability or because they are badly behaved. Poor school work may reflect a rejection of learning and authority rather than absence of talent, and to some extent the schools themselves may be at fault. Teaching may be dull and uninspiring and the pupils, particularly in their last year, may be bored by the apparent irrelevance to their future employment of much that is taught; and boredom may lead to truancy and minor offences. In addition a misfit at school who is an educational failure, or finds difficulty in accepting alien middle class attitudes may become delinquent to make his presence felt.

In a group of 288 delinquents a detailed description of offences is not profitable, since the great variety of acts committed by these boys cannot be satisfactorily classified. There is in any event no obvious educational problem linked with specific types of delinquency and we have therefore grouped them as follows.

(a) Those cautioned by the police for any offence or sentenced by the courts for a non-indictable offence or offences (the trivial offenders);

(b) Those sentenced for not more than one indictable offence whether or not they have also been cautioned or sentenced for trivial offences (the serious offenders);

(c) Those sentenced for more than one indictable offence (the repeaters).

The majority of the trivial offences were infringements of the traffic laws or trespass on railway property, while the majority of the serious offences were breaking and entering or larceny. The division into trivial or serious is not always easy to justify for to the laymen some serious (or indictable) offences appear less important than some trivial (or non-indictable). Separation of these two types of offence has however the advantage of being based on an accepted legal classification which allows comparisons to be made with other studies and this for us outweighed its disadvantages. As already mentioned, these offences are spread over nine years of these boys' lives—not equally however for half occurred after the age of fourteen. Thus the older boys, when in their last year at school or just starting work, are more likely than the younger boys to offend. These are the boys who are mainly concerned in trivial acts; indeed those who come to the notice of the police at an earlier age include the majority of serious offenders and repeaters.

The delinquent boys in this study are not of course evenly scattered throughout the population. The risks of delinquency are higher for the manual working than for middle class boys, but the upper manual working class are only slightly more likely to be delinquent than the lower middle class. The highest risk is in the lower manual working class and it seems that lack of education of the parents or the low interest in education that goes with it is an additional important factor since, even within the lower manual working class, the boys are less likely to become delinquent if their parents had made some attempt to get further education through night classes or correspondence courses after leaving school, even if this attempt had been unsuccessful in producing further qualifications (Douglas, Ross, Hammond and Mulligan, 1966).

Within each social class the parents of delinquent boys stand out as taking little interest in their sons' school work and in being prepared to let them leave school at the earliest opportunity. The mothers of these boys also were conspicuous for their failure to use the available maternity and child welfare services. They were also unfavourably assessed by the health visitors for the standard of care they gave their children and their homes. As the risk of delinquency is greater in the larger families than in the smaller, it is not surprising that many of the homes of offenders were over-crowded, and that more than threequarters never had a bed to themselves up to the time they were eleven years old.*

Broken homes are more common among the delinquent than non-delinquent boys, but it is divorce and separation that are important, the risks of delinquency in these circumstances (23 per cent) being approximately twice as high as expected. Even so threequarters of the sons of divorced or separated parents keep out of trouble. The

* See Table 28.

[119]

chances of delinquency are not increased by the death of a parent (this is usually the father), nor by the father's unemployment owing to illness. Frequent absence of the father from home on account of his work leads to a slightly raised chance of delinquency, but mothers who go out to work are no more likely to have delinquent sons than are mothers who stay at home. Lastly there is only a slight association between periods of early separation of a child from his family and later delinquent behaviour. There is then no clear and simple relationship between delinquency and unstable family life or the break up of the family. The high risk of delinquency among the children of divorced and separated parents suggests however that prolonged emotional tension and disharmony in the home, rather than the loss of a parent, is the contributory cause.

It has been suggested that the risks of delinquency are high among pupils attending Catholic schools but this view is not supported by the present study. Pupils from these schools are no more and no less likely to offend than those attending maintained schools or schools of other denominations. There are however certain types of school and certain school characteristics associated with delinquent behaviour; rather fewer delinquents than expected went to primary schools that had a good past record of success in the secondary selection examinations. Even so, and without allowing for the fact that many delinquents come from large families and from the lower manual working class, the proportion of trivial offenders at grammar schools is similar to that in the secondary modern schools. More serious offenders are however found mainly in the latter. There is no clear relationship between the social class of the majority of pupils at a school and the risk of delinquency. A manual working class boy at a school with largely middle class pupils is no more and no less likely to become delinquent, than if he were in a school which draws its pupils mainly from the manual working classes. In general the characteristics of the secondary schools that we have looked at show a more tenuous relationship with delinquency than we expected.

The primary school records show that, even before they come before the courts, a high proportion of the delinquent boys are poor workers or lazy, lack powers of concentration or are difficult to discipline. In the secondary schools also their teachers report

[120]

adversely on their attitude to work and on their behaviour, both inside and outside the class room. The trivial offenders are the least likely to be picked out as being inattentive and ill behaved, and the serious the most likely. All groups of delinquents have a poor record of school attendance, losing time through many odd days away rather than in long spells, and in this respect the trivial offenders are similar to the serious and repeaters. A history of truancy in the secondary schools however is very closely related not only to delinquent behaviour as a whole but also to its serious-ness: 15 per cent of the trivial offenders compared with 38 per cent of those who came before the courts for more than one serious offence, are truants at some time during their years in the secondary schools, whereas in a population of non-offenders from similar types of home only 10 per cent have a history of truancy during their secondary school years.

When the school records are related to the ages at which the boys offend, it is clear that they are reluctant scholars even before they get into trouble and remain so, even if they do not subsequently appear before the courts.

From what has been said about their attitude to work and behaviour in class, it is to be expected that the delinquents would make low scores in the tests. All groups of offenders have low scores at each age. The trivial and serious offenders reach, on the average, a similar level of test performance, nearly 5 points below the non-delinquent group at fifteen years. The repeaters however are further behind—nearly 9 points.* The test performance of the delinquents was poor even when they were first tested at eight, and there is only a relatively small additional deterioration in the succeeding years. It seems that these boys had educational problems from their earliest days at school. This pattern is similar to that shown by nervous or mixed nervous and aggressive pupils, those with high neuroticism scores and those with several symptoms. It is very different from that shown by the boys who are trouble-some in class—their scores deteriorate substantially over the school period.

Part of the poor performance of delinquents may be explained by home circumstances, but even after allowances have been made

* See Table 29.

[121]

for the size of families from which they come, the social class of their parents, the standards of maternal care and the standards of housing, their test results remain below expectation. The trivial and serious offenders are then approximately 2½ points below and the repeaters 4 points; these differences are only half as large as those observed before the adjustments were made. All delinquents make on the average lower scores in the verbal ability test than in the non-verbal, and the scores of the serious offenders and repeaters in mathematics and reading are also lower than their non-verbal results. The trivial offenders, in contrast do about as well in mathematics and reading tests as in the non-verbal ability.*

In all social classes and in all types of school, the delinquents leave early. From secondary modern schools, 95 per cent have left before the end of the 1961/2 session compared with 81 per cent of the non-delinquents; in the grammar schools, only 53 per cent are still at school at the beginning of the 1962/3 session compared with 74 per cent of the non-delinquents. With these large proportions leaving early, few are in a position to take 'O' levels—only 7 delinquents gained good 'O' level certificates and only 22 a certificate of any kind. Fifteen of these successful candidates were trivial offenders, and none was a repeater.

The high rate of truancy during the secondary school years among the delinquents has been mentioned and it is of some interest to compare the test performance and school records of the truants with the delinquents. These secondary school truants are also pupils who throughout their school careers make low scores in all tests. At fifteen their verbal intelligence test scores are particularly low and their mathematics and reading scores are also depressed compared with their non-verbal intelligence test performance. The truants, as would be expected, leave early whatever type of school they are attending and, as with the delinquents, few attempt the General Certificate 'O' level examinations.

Risks of delinquency and truancy are high among pupils picked out by secondary school teachers as being aggressive or both nervous and aggressive. They are also high among those with many habit symptoms at fifteen.

On the self-rating inventory given at thirteen the delinquents have

* See Table 29.

[122]

high scores for neuroticism, i.e. they pick out the statements relating to anxiety. Those who have high neuroticism scores have a high risk of delinquency, whatever the nature of the teachers' ratings. Thus the pupils classified by the teachers as nervous are three times as likely to be delinquent if they themselves have picked out the neuroticism items. The highest proportions of delinquents, 29 and 28 per cent, are found among the boys with high neuroticism scores who are also rated by the teachers as aggressive or mixed aggressive and nervous. The lowest proportions, 4 and 5 per cent, are found among the nervous, non-neurotics and those who are not picked out as nervous or aggressive by the teachers and have low scores for neuroticism.

The delinquents in summary are badly behaved in form and lack interest in school work; they are likely to be truant, are seen by their teachers as aggressive or both nervous and aggressive, and in their answers to the self-rating inventory show themselves to be anxious. All these characteristics taken individually are also associated with poor school performance, and it is not unexpected to find that the test scores of the delinquents are well below expectation, even after taking account of their family background, family size and housing.

The other characteristic of the delinquents, which is also common to the truants and those with poor behaviour ratings, is that they are poor scholars from the age of eight and perhaps even earlier. In spite of their inattentiveness in class, their excess absences and later truancy, their performance deteriorates only slightly, in relative terms, during their years at school. This would suggest that the reasons for the poor academic performance of delinquents, and also for their lack of involvement in their school work, lie in the pre-school years rather than in their inattention and absence later.

Chapter Seventeen

Family Size and Achievement

When the school performance and test results of boys and girls from different sized families were compared in *The Home and the School*, a number of questions were raised, which may now be re-examined in the light of subsequent information. It was found (as others have found before, e.g. Maxwell, 1961) that those who had many brothers and sisters made, on the average, lower test scores than those who had few. Inadequate home conditions, lack of parental interest and poor schooling, all of which are associated with large families, explained approximately one-third of these differences. However even in the most prosperous homes, where in most instances all the children would be well cared for and adequately fed whatever the size of family, those with many brothers and sisters made lower scores than expected in all the tests. It seemed therefore that there are other more subtle influences at work than the environmental conditions that have just been mentioned.

The unanswered questions from the earlier report on the relationship between the family size and school progress were, first, whether subsequent additions to the family would alter the degree of association. It was thought possible that late births to parents who had carefully planned their families—and so would be likely to be relatively intelligent—would add children of high ability to the larger families and so improve their average test performance. If so, the gap in measured ability between the large and small families would be reduced. Second, it had been noticed that between eight and eleven years there was no divergence of the test scores of children in large and in small families—this suggested that the main effects of family size on intelligence and attainment occurred during the pre-

[124]

school as opposed to the school years; this would be confirmed if there was no subsequent change. The third question concerned the nature of the handicaps of children from large families—in which tests were their scores especially low?

At the end of the primary school years, the boys and girls from small families gained more places at grammar schools than those from large. This was explained by their higher measured ability. It remained to be seen if those from small families excelled also in the General Certificate examinations, and stayed on longer at school. If so, was this simply a reflection of their higher scores in the ability and attainment tests, or had they an advantage over and above that predicted from their ability?

During the four years, 1957–1961, there was a number of additional births in the Survey families, a high proportion of them being in those that were already large. The relationship between test performance and family size has not been altered by these additional births, and it seems that the families were sufficiently near completion by the time the children were eleven for the full effects of family size to show themselves. This does not mean however that it would have been satisfactory to take family size at an earlier age; if for example it had been taken when the Survey members were six or eight years old, rather than at eleven or fifteen, the association with test performance would have been exaggerated.

There was, as already mentioned, no change in the relative test performance of children from large and small families between the ages of eight and eleven; and at fifteen years also, the children from small families have an advantage that is similar to those recorded earlier. When manual working class children are considered separately, the smallest difference between test performance of those from different sized families is found at fifteen years, and the largest at eight, while for the middle class children, there is little relative change from one age to another.*

If the effects of family size on test performance stemmed largely from poor environmental conditions, the children from large families would be expected to become progressively handicapped as they grew older. This as we have seen is not so; indeed in the manual working classes there is a suggestion that the opposite holds. This

* See Table 30.

[125]

confirms the earlier suggestion that the low measured ability of children from large families is determined by factors that exert their effect before the age at which they start school.

Family size differences are smallest in the non-verbal test of intelligence and largest in the attainment tests. It is moreover particularly in vocabulary that those from large families are handicapped. At both eight and eleven years, those with three or more brothers and sisters make scores in tests of vocabulary that are 8 points below those made by only children, whereas in mechanical reading they are only 5 points behind. Unfortunately there was no direct measure of vocabulary in the fifteen year tests, but the reading test was of the sentence completion type, assessing the understanding of words, as well as the pupil's ability to read. The boys and girls from large families are 7 points behind the only children in this test, whereas they are only 5 points behind them in mathematics and 3 points in non-verbal intelligence. There is therefore consistent evidence that it is particularly in the understanding and use of words that boys and girls from large families are handicapped. This handicap is as evident at eight as later. It is probable that the growth of vocabulary is affected by the extent to which children, when learning to talk, come into contact with other pre-school children whose small vocabularies and elementary grammar offer little verbal stimulation.

The following account of the influence of early experience on test performance is confined to children from middle class families for the reason that verbal stimulation from adults, when present, will be at a high level. In these families moreover there is relatively little deterioration in living conditions, even when births are closely spaced. In each size of middle class family, the vocabulary scores of the children are relatively high when births are widely spaced and relatively low when they are close together. Table 31 shows the test scores of middle class children with two brothers or sisters after they have been grouped by the number of pre-school children in the family during the first four years of their lives. There is little difference in the average scores made by these boys and girls in the non-verbal tests but their vocabulary scores fall as the number of other small children in the family increases and so do their scores in the fifteen year reading test.

Much has been written about the acquisition of language in the

[126]

manual working class, and how the small vocabulary used by the parents and the crude grammatical constructions of the sentences spoken, restrict children's ability to express themselves precisely and effectively in words (e.g. Bernstein, 1965). We would suggest that insufficient attention has been paid to the lack of verbal stimulation that may result when a child, during the years when he is learning to speak, spends much of his time with others near his own age and models his language on theirs. The Plowden Committee (Central Advisory Council, 1967) advocated the extension of nursery school education implicitly to counter, amongst other things, the lack of verbal stimulation found in some families. But unless the proportion of nursery staff is high enough for the children to be able to talk and discuss constantly with adults, the already restricted child may suffer further impairment in language development through being thrown into even longer and more intimate association with others of his own age.

Not all test scores decline regularly with each increase in family size. In the middle classes, for example the mathematics scores of the fifteen year olds show little decline in passing from families of one to those of two or three children. This is owing to the unusual pattern of results found for the middle class boys, whose mathematics scores are actually higher in families of two or three, than they are for only children. In contrast, the average mathematics scores of the middle class girls fall with each increase in family size. In view of the generally poor performance of girls in mathematics it is of some interest that the middle class girls who are only children score as highly in the mathematics test as do the only boys. With larger families however the mathematics performance of the girls falls progressively behind that of the boys.

In the General Certificate examinations boys and girls from large families are less successful than those from small. They get fewer certificates and at a lower level. This however is largely owing to their lower measured ability and when allowances are made for this, it is solely those with three or more brothers or sisters who are at a disadvantage. Indeed at each level of measured ability, except the highest, the only children get fewer good certificates than those from either two or three child families.

Children from two child families stay on approximately as long

[127]

at school as only children, but with the larger families, there is a considerable decrease in the length of school life: this is particularly evident at the lower levels of ability.* For example among children of just below average ability, 29 per cent of those from two child families completed the 1961/2 session but only 14 per cent from families of four or more. This is partly explained by the higher proportion of manual working class, particularly lower manual working class, families that are large. But even in the middle classes there is a tendency for the children from large families to leave early.

It might have been expected that the youngest boys and girls would stay on longer at school, since family expenses would by then be reduced, and the older ones would be contributing to the household expenses. This does not however occur—indeed in the borderline group of ability, the youngest in each size of family leave earlier than either the middle or the eldest. This suggests that finance is not the only reason for early leaving among boys and girls from large families, and that the provision of grants to make up for the earnings forgone by pupils who stay on at school might not help those for whom it was meant.

* See Table 32.

[128]

Chapter Eighteen

Birth Order and Spacing

In the last chapter it was mentioned that, at certain levels of ability, children with one brother or sister did better in the General Certificate of Education examinations, and left school later, than only children. In the middle classes moreover boys from two or three child families made higher scores in mathematics than boys who were only children. These observations encouraged us to look more closely at the extent to which position in the family, sex of the other children and birth spacing influence academic performance.

A comparison of the educational progress of elder and younger children at the ages of eight and eleven was given in *The Home and the School*. It suggested that the first-born were spurred on by competition with their younger brothers and sisters and that in consequence they gained more selective secondary school places than would have been expected from their measured ability. At this stage however no account was taken of the sex of the other children, or of the length of the interval between births. These additional aspects of family structure are discussed in this chapter mainly with reference to two child families. The complexity of the relationships in the larger families—with three children there are 24 different combinations of sex and birth rank into which an individual child may fall, even before account is taken of birth spacing—made it impracticable to examine them satisfactorily in a sample of this size. Indeed even when discussion is limited to those in two child families, numerical restrictions are serious.

Boys and girls are grouped in the following discussion by whether they were first- or last-born, by whether they have a brother or a sister, and by the length of the interval between their own birth

[129]

and that of their sib. No attempt is made to disentangle the over-lapping effects of each factor on the others.

The first comparison we make is between the elder and younger boys. At each age the elder boys have higher average scores than the younger and are as much above them at eight as at fifteen. This is the average picture for all tests. In the non-verbal test at each of these ages, the elder and younger boys are not differentiated; the younger have a very slight advantage at eleven, but not at the other two years. In all reading tests however and to a lesser extent in mathematics and verbal intelligence, the elder boys have a considerable advantage over the younger; they are 2·9 points ahead in reading at eight and maintain this lead thereafter.* In reading and mathematics, the elder boys are also above the boys who are *only* children, though in non-verbal ability they are below. From this it seems unlikely that the advantage of the elder boys is associated with more frequent and prolonged contacts with parents and other adults in early life, or from early attempts to interest them in learning. The pattern of their scores, namely high achievement in the attainment tests as opposed to non-verbal intelligence, is set at eight and does not change thereafter.

The elder do consistently better than both the younger and the only boys in the General Certificate examinations and stay on longer at school. Their superiority is greatest in the proportion gaining good certificates—30 per cent, compared with 21 per cent of the younger and 20 per cent of the only boys, a result which would not have been expected from a comparison of their scores in the non-verbal intelligence tests. In their aspirations for entering full-time higher education on leaving school the elder boys are also considerably more ambitious.† Among those of high ability, 80 per cent wish to continue with full-time education, compared with 59 per cent of the younger, and 61 per cent of the only. In contrast the views of both teachers and mothers are similar whether they are referring to the elder, younger or only.

When in addition to the boy's position in the family, the sex of the other child is taken into account, there is little alteration in the pattern of differences in the tests, General Certificate results, or

* See Table 33.
† See Table 34.

[130]

leaving, already described. The elder are consistently superior whether they have a brother or a sister. Those who have elder sisters however make lower scores than the rest of the boys from two child families; at eleven for example they are 2·3 points of test score below those with elder brothers and 4·0 points below boys with younger sisters. At fifteen they are still below the rest in each type of test.

The higher achievement of the elder boys is not associated with markedly different attitudes to work or substantially greater encouragement from their parents. However slightly more were assessed as hard working at primary school and slightly more had parents who showed a high level of interest in their school work; but these differences are small and can hardly explain the considerably better performance and higher aspirations of the elder boys.

The elder with younger brothers are given more favourable ratings for out of class behaviour than any other group. They are less likely to be rated as nervous or aggressive by the teachers, less likely to have high symptom counts and less likely to choose items relating to anxiety and fears from the self-rating inventory.

Similar comparisons show no substantial differences in educational progress between elder and younger girls, though at each age and in each test the younger have rather higher average scores than the elder. Owing to its consistency this cannot be ignored, though it is more tenuous than the reverse relationship already described for the boys. For girls it would seem that the presence of another child has a favourable effect on the younger rather than the elder. Apart from these differences in test score there is no evidence that the younger girls are academically more successful— their General Certificate results are similar to those of the elder girls, and they are no more likely to stay on at school or to express a wish to enter higher education after leaving school. Neither in their attitude to work nor in the ratings made of their behaviour are there any substantial or consistent differences between elder and younger girls.

The clear differences between elder and younger boys in two child families, and the relative lack of difference between elder and younger girls made it desirable to see whether these findings were paralleled in similar comparisons between children in three child families. The relatively high achievement of first-born boys from two child families is in fact matched by those in families of three. The first-born* boys in these larger families have at each age an advantage over the second-born boys. At eight and fifteen the difference in aggregate test score between the eldest and the second-born boys is similar to that recorded for the difference between elder and younger boys in families of two. The individual tests at fifteen show the same pattern; in the non-verbal test the elder boy makes a slightly lower score than the younger; the eldest in families of three also makes a slightly lower score than the second. In all the other tests the first-born boy is at an advantage. The test performance of the youngest boys in families of three closely approximates that of the second-born boys and is well below the performance of the eldest. Here again it is in the attainment tests that the youngest boy is at a disadvantage.

For the girls in three child families no clear pattern emerges.

The last factor to be considered is the spacing of births. The following three groups of intervals for children in two child families are chosen largely on the basis of the numbers available: (a) short intervals following or preceeding the birth of two years or less, (b) medium intervals of two to four years, (c) long intervals of more than four years. The test scores of boys and girls from two child families grouped in this way show remarkably consistent differences in which the highest scores, at each age, are made by those with medium birth intervals. There is no evidence however that those with medium birth intervals increase their lead in the attainment tests between eight and fifteen years, and the effect of birth spacing on performance seems to be fully established by the age of eight, when they were first tested. The advantage of those with medium birth intervals is similar for both boys and girls, and for both elder and younger; it is smallest in the non-verbal tests of intelligence and greatest in the attainment tests, particularly in mathematics, for the boys.†

The advantage of those who have medium birth intervals extends to their performance in the General Certificate of Education. They

* We refer here to the eldest child in the family.
† See Table 35.

[132]

get more certificates than those with either shorter or longer intervals and more of these are at a high level. They are also more likely to stay on at school.* Their better educational performance is partly explained by their higher ability but, even after allowing for this, they are still superior. In view of this high standard of performance, it is surprising that at neither the primary nor the secondary schools are the boys or girls with medium birth intervals picked out as working harder than the rest, though for the boys higher levels of parental interest are recorded.

It might be argued that the more intelligent parents would be likely to choose intervals of two or four years between births, as being best for both the mother and the child, and plan their families accordingly. There is some evidence for this. The proportion of two child families, with medium birth spacing is 45 per cent in the middle class and 30 per cent in the manual working class. Within each social class however the same relationship between attainment scores and birth spacing holds. While we cannot dismiss the possibility that the superiority associated with birth spacings of two to four years may be an artifact of family planning, it is unlikely to be wholly so.

Finally there is no relation between birth spacing and unusual behaviour, such as aggressiveness or nervousness, habit symptoms or self-reported anxiety.

The results of this study of the structure of two child families related to educational progress lead to the following conclusions. The elder boys do better than their younger sibs, either brothers or sisters, and show high educational achievement and aspirations. There is no evidence that they suffer from competition with a younger sib; indeed in the ratings made by teachers, mothers and the boys themselves, they show up favourably compared with their younger brothers or sisters. With the girls such relatively small differences as there are in test performance favour the younger; in General Certificate results and in leaving however there is no difference between elder and younger girls. These findings in two child families are wholly supported by those in three child families, where the equivalent positions are the eldest and the second-born child. Medium birth intervals of 2 to 4 years are the most favourable

* See Table 36.

[133]

when judged by the educational performance of both the boys and the girls. This is partly, though probably not wholly, explained by social class differences in family planning. The effects of both position in the family and birth spacing are fully developed by the time the children are eight years old and may be regarded as being acquired during the pre-school years.

For a study of family structure the National Survey falls short of what is desirable; it is too small for a rigorous statistical examination of the overlapping effects of the rather simple factors we are able to examine, and it is too large and too widely dispersed to permit the detailed exploration of family relationships that is necessary to interpret the interactions between parental attitudes, jealousy and rivalry on the one hand, and family structure on the other. It is hoped however that these results will help to focus further attention on an interesting and important field of research.

Chapter Nineteen

Adolescence

During the whole of the secondary school period and, for girls, during the last years at primary school, children of the same age show wide differences in their stage of sexual maturity. A very few girls are sexually mature in the primary schools and, at the other extreme, a few are not yet mature when they enter the sixth forms of secondary schools. For boys, who on the average reach sexual maturity two years later than the girls, there is a similar range in the speed of sexual development. These simple physiological facts raise problems which vary from the purely educational, to the need to provide facilities for the few girls who reach puberty while they are at primary schools, and to help and advise the increasing number of girls who become pregnant while they are still at school. In 1941, 220 girls under the age of sixteen had babies compared with 1,131 girls 21 years later (Department of Education and Science, 1964).

The increase in births to schoolgirls underlines an interesting and largely unexplained trend, namely that the average age at which boys and girls reach puberty has been getting earlier. It seems that over the last century the age at which children reach puberty has advanced by 4 months every 10 years, and girls who today are sexually mature at the age of thirteen, would not have reached puberty until they were fifteen if they had been born at the turn of the century. Boys also may have had the same advancement of puberty but this is not certain owing to the difficulties of measuring their stage of sexual development. Recent studies of London schoolboys however strongly suggest this to be so. For the girls there is no sign that this trend towards early puberty is slowing up, though it is hard to believe that it will not do so soon. It should be

[135]

remembered of course that some girls, who are in no other way abnormal, start their periods at ten or earlier. If the spread of ages at which children reach puberty is being reduced, i.e. if children are becoming more uniform in their rates of sexual development as might be expected from their more uniform home circumstances and nutrition, the average age of puberty could be much further reduced while still remaining within the present range of normality. This trend towards earlier puberty, if it continues, will lead to a more mature and physically more uniform sixth form. It will also add to the problems at the primary school level and raise even more acutely than today the questions of whether allowances should be made for developmental as well as chronological age when selecting, grouping or streaming pupils at various stages of their school careers.

It has long been thought that the sexually more mature boys and girls have an advantage in any selection process. This would be educationally undesirable if, as some suspect, the later maturing pupils were to catch up as they themselves reached puberty. This view is based on the assumption that there is a pre-pubertal spurt in intelligence similar to the well known spurt in growth. The tentative findings reported for the National Survey girls at eleven did not support it. The early maturing girls, it is true, made higher scores in tests of ability and attainment, but their advantage over the late maturers was as great at eight years (that is to say before they showed any sign of approaching puberty) as at eleven. Now that these young people are older, a fuller examination of the question is feasible and can be extended to the boys as well as the girls.

The girls are grouped by the age at which they had their first period (age of menarche) into the following four groups.

(a) Very early menarche (before eleven years ten months);
(b) Early menarche (eleven years ten months and before twelve years ten months);
(c) Late menarche (twelve years ten months and before thirteen years ten months);
(d) Very late menarche (thirteen years ten months or later).

The earliest age at which a girl in this study was reported to have started her periods is eight years; at eleven years, 1·4 per cent of the

[136]

girls had started their periods, 15 per cent had enlarged breasts and pigmented pubic hair and a further 30 per cent had some breast enlargement. This means that nearly half the girls who were about to leave primary school showed some sign of advancing puberty. It was not however until thirteen years two months that half had reached menarche.

The boys have been grouped by the doctors' description at the fifteen year old medical examination of genitals, voice and the presence and profuseness of axillary and pubic hair. The following four groups are used (See Appendix IV).

(a) Mature boys;
(b) Boys with advanced signs of puberty;
(c) Boys with early signs of puberty;
(d) Infantile boys.

We try to answer two questions in this chapter. First what are the main characteristics of the boys and girls who reach puberty early or late, and second how much (if at all) do the early maturers differ from the later maturers in their school work and examination results? The answer to the first question is needed to interpret the answer to the second—if the early maturers differ in their school achievement from the late, is this because they come from different types of family or is it a result of their different rates of physical, mental or emotional growth?

There is no doubt that in the last century menarche was earlier among the daughters of the well-to-do than of the poor. Tanner (1955) for example quotes a study which showed that in Manchester, in about 1820, educated ladies reached menarche just over a year in advance of working women. And Marro (1900) at the end of the nineteenth century gave distributions of menarche for Piedmontese girls which showed the same difference between rich and poor. In the underdeveloped countries today there is also evidence of a similar difference in the age of maturation.

It has been pointed out that grammar school girls reach puberty at an earlier age than secondary modern school girls, though for reasons that will be evident later, this is adequately explained by what happens at the time of secondary selection and cannot be taken as evidence of an association between poverty and delayed sexual maturation.

[137]

In the present study, the age of reaching puberty is similar in each social class—the very small excess of early maturing children in the middle class being adequately explained by a relationship with family size which will shortly be described. This unexpected finding is supported by other recent evidence from Aberdeen (Nisbet and Illsley, 1963) and Bristol (Rogan, 1958) and it seems that at some time during this century economic factors in Britain ceased to exert a differential influence on the age of onset of puberty. When this occurred is unknown as there are no regularly collected records of sexual maturation which can be linked to the type of family from which the pupils come. This is a serious defect in the school medical records which it is hoped will be remedied in the future, though there are difficulties in collecting this type of information routinely in a comparable way throughout the country.

It is well known that children from small families reach puberty on the average at a younger age than children from large. This is evident in the present study where, at the age of twelve years ten months, 51 per cent of the girls with no brothers or sisters have reached menarche, compared with 31 per cent of those with four or more. Put another way, half the girls reach menarche at or before ·twelve years nine months if they are only children and seven months later than this if they are members of large families. The same sort of relationship holds for the boys.

The next question is whether the rate of development of first-born children is similar to that of only children or to that of their own brothers and sisters—is it in other words the position in the family or the size of the family that matters? If the former, then there would be a strong suggestion that intra-uterine events had an influence in setting the rate of sexual development. If family size rather than position is important then events occurring after birth would be involved. When the level of maturity of first-born children is related to the size of their family, it is clear that, for the boys, size is the important influence. In reaching puberty the only boy is as much ahead of the eldest of three as he is ahead of the middle or youngest. For the girls the main difference is between the only children and the rest.*

* For a discussion of the relation between family size and puberty see Douglas (1965).

[138]

At birth there is no difference in the weight of early and late maturing children once allowances have been made for the size of family into which they are born. The early maturing boys and girls cut their teeth and start to sit up, stand, walk and talk at the same ages as the late maturers but they are weaned on to solid food at a rather younger age. By two years, both the boys and girls are ordered by height, those in the earliest maturing group being on the average the tallest and those in the latest maturing group the smallest. This order is maintained and the differences between the groups increase during the succeeding years. It is likely however that the late maturing boys and girls who continue to grow in height after the early maturers have stopped will end up the tallest. Indeed for the girls at fifteen, when threequarters are mature, this has already happened, and the orderly arrangement of average heights seen at the earlier ages, is no longer found. As the majority of boys at fifteen have not reached puberty there is still a wide range at this age between the average heights of the infantile and the fully mature boys (see Diagram III).

The growth of these boys and girls has been described in some detail so as to illustrate the early age at which the various puberty groups are differentiated from each other, and to indicate the sort of educational problems that would be set if the rate of development of mental ability followed similar lines to the rate of physical.

Before going on to describe the relationship of onset of puberty to educational performance, it should be mentioned that many social and biological characteristics of these children and their parents have been examined to try to establish associations with early or late puberty. The only substantial relationship is found with family size and crowding of births. It seems that in interpreting the following account of their school progress, it is sufficient to remember that the early maturing boys and girls, on the average, come from smaller families than the late maturing ones and that this gives them an educational advantage.

The aggregate mean test scores at eight, eleven and fifteen are shown in Diagram IV for boys and girls in each of the four maturity groups. The scores at each age refer to the same pupils and of course each boy and girl stays throughout in the same group. During these seven years, there has been a relatively constant difference

[139]

between the average test performance of pupils in the extreme groups.

At eight years, and well before any of the boys had shown signs of puberty, those who were later to be assessed as mature at fifteen

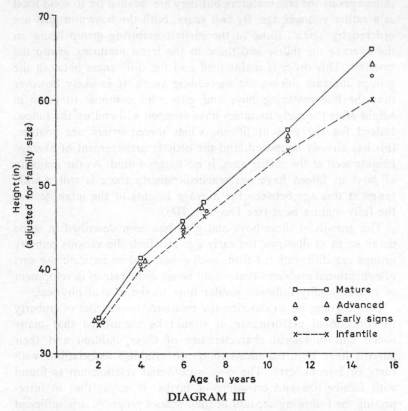

DIAGRAM III

The average height of boys at two, four, six, seven, eleven and fifteen years grouped by their stage of puberty at fifteen years.

scored 4·8 points more than those who were later to be assessed as infantile. At fifteen, the gap between them was 4·1 points. Similarly the girls who reached menarche before eleven years ten months scored in the eight year tests an average of 3·2 points more than those who reached menarche after fourteen years, and in the fifteen year tests they scored 3·7 points more. There is no suggestion here of a spurt in intelligence or attainment to match the pre-pubertal spurt in physical growth. The intermediate groups follow a rather puzzling pattern. At eight, the advanced boys score

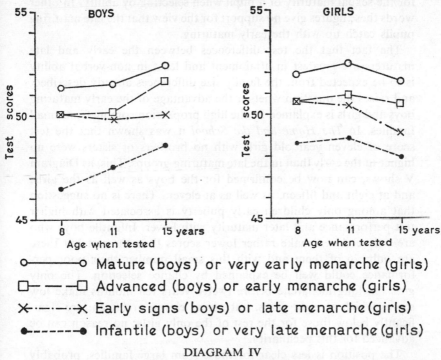

o———o Mature (boys) or very early menarche (girls)

□— —□ Advanced (boys) or early menarche (girls)

✕·—·—✕ Early signs (boys) or late menarche (girls)

●------● Infantile (boys) or very late menarche (girls)

DIAGRAM IV

The aggregate test scores at eight, eleven and fifteen years of boys and girls grouped by their stage of puberty.

exactly the same as those with early signs; during the next seven years the two groups diverge, so that by fifteen there is a difference of 1·6 points in favour of the more mature. Similarly the girls reaching menarche between eleven years ten months and twelve years ten months make exactly the same scores at eight years as the girls reaching menarche between thirteen and fourteen, whereas at fifteen they are 1·4 points ahead.

Similar patterns of performance are found in each of the individual tests though the differences in average scores between the early

[141]

and late maturers are greater in the attainment than in the intelligence tests. In none of the tests is there any tendency for the late maturing pupils to catch up with the early and, up to the age of fifteen at any rate, it appears that there is no need to make allowances for the sexual maturity of a pupil when selecting by ability. In other words these figures give no support for the view that the late maturing pupils catch up with the early maturing.

The fact that the test differences between the early and late maturers are greatest in attainment and least in non-verbal ability is to be expected from the family size differences already described, and raises the question whether the advantage of the early maturing boys and girls is explained by the high proportion coming from small families. In *The Home and the School* it was shown that the test score of eleven year old girls with no brothers or sisters were no higher in the early than in the late maturing groups. This, as Diagram V shows, can now be confirmed for the boys as well as the girls, and at eight and fifteen, as well as at eleven. There is no suggestion that among only children early puberty is associated with higher test performance and later maturity with lower. Infantile boys who are only children make rather lower scores than the rest but there are only 26 of them and with this small number their poor performance could well be explained by chance selection. The only girls reaching menarche before twelve years ten months make low scores which at eight years, but not at eleven or fifteen, are significantly below those for the rest of the only girls; no reason can be advanced for this peculiarity.

The position is less clear for those from large families, probably because there are complicating factors such as position in family and birth spacing to take into account. In each size of family taken separately, the differences in average scores of the early and late maturers persist, but are less than when the sample is taken as a whole. We consider the only children provide the critical case; if there is no association between stage of puberty and test performance in only children, then it is unlikely that there is a meaningful association between them in the larger families.

It was shown in the previous book that the early maturing girls were more likely than the late to be allocated to selective schools; this however was no more than would be expected from their higher ability. As more of these were at grammar and other selective schools, it would be expected that more of the mature pupils would stay at school to start the 1962/3 session, and this is indeed so if the whole population is taken together. At each level of ability however

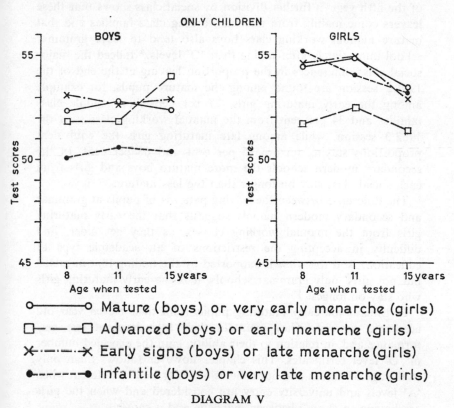

ONLY CHILDREN

BOYS   GIRLS

○———○ Mature (boys) or very early menarche (girls)
□— — —□ Advanced (boys) or early menarche (girls)
✗—·—·—✗ Early signs (boys) or late menarche (girls)
●-------● Infantile (boys) or very late menarche (girls)

DIAGRAM V

The aggregate test scores at eight, eleven and fifteen years of boys and girls, who are only children, grouped by their stage of puberty.

similar proportions of early and late maturing pupils stay on and there is no need to introduce any further factor of emotional or intellectual maturity to explain the longer school life of the early maturers taken as a group. The results of the 'O' level examinations

[143]

show a similar pattern, the early maturers gaining more 'O' levels and at a higher standard than the rest, though this is largely explained by their superior ability at fifteen.

In the selective schools though not in the group as a whole, an unexpectedly high proportion of the mature girls leave at the end of the fifth year; a further division by social class shows that these leavers come mainly from manual working class families and that mature manual working class boys also tend to leave grammar school immediately after taking their 'O' levels.* Indeed the major social class differences in the proportion leaving at the end of the 1961/2 session are found among the mature pupils, for example among the early maturing girls, 77 per cent from middle class families and 34 per cent from the manual working class start the 1962/3 session, while among late maturing girls the equivalent proportions staying on are 75 per cent and 63 per cent. In the secondary modern schools the more mature boys and girls from each social class stay on longer than the less mature.

The difference between the leaving patterns of pupils at grammar and secondary modern schools suggests that the early maturing girls from the manual working classes, as they get older, find difficulty in accepting the restrictions of an academic type of education. And this view is supported by the finding that in mixed but not girls' only grammar schools, it is the early maturing girls who stay on longest.†

In general the early maturing pupils fulfil their eleven year old academic promise. They maintain their high level of test performance and, in relation to their ability, gain the expected number of 'O' level certificates. This chapter however follows them only to the age of sixteen and our conclusions may well be different when 'A' levels and university entry are considered and when the girls are having to choose between marriage and a career.

* See Table 37.
† See Table 17.

[144]

Part IV

Special Studies

Chapter Twenty

Right- and Left-Handedness

Less importance is placed today than in the past on left-handedness as a source of educational and emotional disturbance, but it is still commonly supposed that many children with reading difficulties have weak lateralization of hand and foot, and that a rather high proportion of them are left-eyed. Published results are however conflicting; some report an association between hand and eye preferences and various abnormalities of learning and behaviour, others show none at all.

In a study of 78 children of average intelligence who had developmental aphasia (Ingram and Reid, 1956), only 11 per cent were right-handed, though an additional 35 per cent had slight preferences for using their right hand. This group of children had other unusual characteristics; many came from broken homes and many showed behaviour and personality disturbances. A high proportion of their parents were themselves in need of psychiatric help and nearly half were over-anxious about their children's educational attainment. The wide range of peculiarities of these children and the parents suggests that there was selective referral to the clinic from the schools.

Left-handedness interferes with the ordinary tasks of the classroom, and many believe that left-handed children, if forced to write with their right hand, may develop a stammer or become emotionally disturbed. It has been said that 'no question is put by the teachers to the school psychiatrists more frequently than "how should I deal with a left-handed pupil?" ' (Burt, 1958); indeed this may be an additional incentive for referring children with educational or emotional difficulties for medical advice.

Information on hand and eye preferences was obtained during special medical examinations when the National Survey boys and girls were six and eleven years. At the six year examination, the doctors recorded which hand the child used when writing or drawing, and at the eleven year examination the child was also asked to pick up a ball placed directly in front of him, and throw it into a box, note being taken of the hand or hands used. With this information, the boys and girls have been grouped as consistently right-handed in both years, as consistently left-handed or as having mixed or inconsistent hand preferences. A more detailed classification of the nature of the inconsistent hand preferences is not profitable owing to the relatively small number in each sub-group. Passing mention is however made of the few boys and girls who between six and eleven years changed their writing hand.

In addition to recording the hand used by the pupils for various tasks, the school doctors also tested at each age the eye used for sighting objects.

Seven per cent of the boys and 5 per cent of the girls consistently used their left hands for writing, drawing and picking up a ball, and 10 per cent of both boys and girls were inconsistent in their hand preferences. There is no evidence of the attitude taken by either the teachers or the parents to the use of the left hand, but it is likely that the majority of the left-handed and the inconsistent were at some stage encouraged, if not persuaded, to use their right hands. The proportion of non-right-handers recorded in this sample at both medical examinations is therefore likely to be smaller than would have been found if the testing had been at a younger age.

In the past, pressures to change from the left to the right hand seem to have been frequent and effective, and it is probable that the parents and teachers of this group of pupils similarly encouraged the use of the right hand. Sir Cyril Burt, writing in 1953, recommended that right-handed training should begin at the earliest possible age. He suggested that left-handed children should be given plenty of preliminary practice in the use of their right hands before they were trained to write with them, and that the change in the use of their hands should be as unconscious as possible. The pressures to use the right hand rather than the left, should be stage-managed so that the right hand is adopted naturally and mechanically.

[148]

That there has been relatively little recent change in attitude towards left-handedness, or rather in the effectiveness of the pressures on left-handers to use their right hands, is suggested by the close similarity of our figures of left-handedness to those published in 1921, which showed 6 per cent of boys and 4 per cent of girls as being left-handed (Burt, 1958).

The hand preferences of 3,253 boys and girls in the educational sample are known. Two relatively small but statistically significant social class differences should be noted. First, a higher proportion of manual working than of middle class boys have inconsistent hand preferences; second, more of the manual working class boys than girls are left-handed or inconsistent in their preferences. The middle class boys and girls have similar hand preferences. This suggests that handedness at eleven years is to some extent socially or culturally determined, and here is a source of selective bias to explain why some studies show sex differences in hand preferences while others do not.

The left-handed and inconsistently handed pupils do as well as the right-handed in the aggregate tests at each age and the same holds for the individual test scores at fifteen. The left-handers are above the rest in their performance in the mathematics and reading tests, and those with inconsistent hand preferences are at a slight disadvantage in the non-verbal test. None of these differences however is statistically significant.

It has often been reported that disturbed hand preferences are commoner among the duller children than among the average, and commoner among the average children than the clever. This partly holds in the present sample. There is no substantial change in hand preferences in passing from the group of boys and girls within one standard deviation of the mean to those of high ability. But among those of relatively low ability (i.e. scoring less than 40 in the aggregate of all tests at fifteen) a significant excess have inconsistent hand preferences. This is so for each type of test but is statistically significant for the mathematics test only.

The fact that there are more pupils with inconsistent hand preferences among those of low ability does not mean that there is a casual connection between the two. It has already been noted that there are more manual working class pupils than middle class with

[149]

mixed-hand preferences. The working class pupils do less well in tests and are in excess among those in the lowest range of ability; for example among the duller boys and girls there are only 58 middle class as compared with 340 manual working class, whereas among the pupils of high ability, there are 403 middle and only 256 manual working class. When corrections are made for the higher proportion of manual working class pupils, in the low ability group, the association of poor performance with inconsistent hand preferences fall well below the level of statistical significance.

It has been suggested that there are more pupils with inconsistent hand preferences among the dull because they are equally clumsy with right and left hands rather than equally skilled. There is no evidence from the present study to support this. Boys and girls with inconsistent hand preferences who make low scores in the tests do not emerge as clumsy when their co-ordination is assessed by hopping, threading needles and picking up objects of different size. Only two of them failed in any of these co-ordination tests given by the school medical officers at the special school examinations at the age of fifteen.

There is little in this study to suggest that the pupils with disturbed lateral preferences are poorer readers—indeed they make rather higher scores in the reading test than would be expected from their performance in the non-verbal intelligence test at fifteen years. The association of reading difficulties with disturbed lateral preferences has however been so heavily emphasized in the past that it is desirable to look in greater detail at the reading performance of these pupils.

Difficulties in reading might have been overcome by the age of fifteen, and so we looked at earlier ages. At eight years, the right-handed boys and girls make slightly higher scores in the reading tests than either the left or the inconsistently handed—a non-significant difference in the expected direction. Further information on reading difficulties comes from the teachers who were asked, when these pupils were ten years of age, to list any outstandingly weak school subjects. They picked out 202 boys and girls as being poor readers. Of these 13 per cent were inconsistent in their hand preferences compared with an expected 10 per cent; this difference is again in the expected direction though not statistically significant.

[150]

It is put into focus by saying that of 367 pupils with inconsistent hand preferences, 27 were regarded by their teachers as being bad readers compared with an expected 20. This slight excess is explained, for the most part, by the relatively high proportion of manual working class pupils who are inconsistently handed.

There are 26 boys and girls who wrote with their right hand at six years, but 5 years later were reported to be using their left. There are also 19 who originally wrote with the left hand but changed to the right. A closer look at these two small groups seemed worth while.

Those who were writing with their right hand at six years but changed later, were slightly below average in test score at eight years; in subsequent tests they improved their scores and at fifteen scored at the expected level. Those who were left-handed originally were also below average at eight years but had deteriorated by a further 2 points in the fifteen year tests. These results are pointers only, but interesting ones. Were those who changed from their right to their left hand really reverting to their preferred hand? Were those changing from their left to their right hand under pressure to do so?

Children who are inconsistent in their hand preferences are said to be more emotionally disturbed and more likely to stammer than children who are wholly right- or wholly left-handed. Further it has been suggested that children who are ambidextrous have difficulties at school which produce stress followed by anxiety and a variety of symptoms of emotional disturbance such as night terrors, enuresis, truancy and pilfering. It has also been said that half of all stutters are ambidextrous, and that when stuttering occurs in a left-handed child who has been forced to use his right hand, especially for writing, a return to left-handedness often produces a great improvement. In the present study there is no evidence that pupils who are left-handed or who have inconsistent hand preferences are emotionally disturbed, stutter or have other speech defects.

Only 50 per cent of the right-handed pupils with perfect vision in both eyes used their right eye when sighting an object in the medical examinations, and this proportion is substantially the same for boys and girls, and for middle class and manual working class. Among all the right-handed pupils, those who use their right eye do slightly better in the tests than those who use their left, or who have no dominant eye and this advantage increases over the years. At eight there are no significant differences in the test scores but at both eleven and fifteen the right-eyed are significantly above those with no fixed eye preference. There are no differences in the test scores of the three groups of middle class boys and girls (those using their left or either eye do just as well as those using their right). In the manual working class however the expected pattern emerges— the right-handed and right-eyed having the highest average score. The fact that there is no difference in the middle class suggests that such discrepancies as are found in the manual working class do not express a direct relationship between eye preference and intelligence or attainment. One explanation is that the less intelligent pupils have more difficulty in understanding the instructions for the sighting test in the first place and therefore are less likely to do the test correctly.

The findings of this chapter show no difference in attainment between the right-, the left- and the inconsistently-handed. The moral to be drawn is one of common sense: encourage but do not force your child in a right-handed world to conform; if he is persistently left-handed however do not worry about his progress or adjustment as he is likely to do just as well as his right-handed class-mates.

Chapter Twenty-one

Short Sight

It is widely believed that university students, scholarship winners and those in jobs which require high standards of intellectual ability are more likely to be short-sighted than others in the general population. This belief is however based for the most part on general impressions rather than on statistical observations, and the apparent association of short sight with high ability may do no more than reflect the fact that able children have parents who, on the whole, are more intelligent and more educationally ambitious than the general run, and so are not only more aware of the importance of correcting defective vision in their children but also have a stronger incentive to do so.

Short sight often develops during the school years, at a time when children are concentrating on near work. In the past it was thought that the process of adapting the lens of the eye for near vision might be associated with the development of short sight, the clever pupils and those excessively addicted to reading over-straining their eyes and impairing their vision. There is no convincing evidence however that near work predisposes to short sight, and there is no physiological reason why this should be. Many today believe that short-sighted pupils do well at school because they find reading and close work easy and because, to a greater or lesser extent, their defective sight prevents them from taking a full and active part in games and other outside activities; in order to compensate for this they strive to succeed in school.

In the social context it has been suggested that short sight is more commonly found in the upper social classes and, in succeeding generations, will become increasingly concentrated there (Jahoda,

1962). The argument runs that short-sighted parents tend to have short-sighted children and those who are short-sighted, being also on the average of superior ability, are likely to be attracted to academic or clerical work and so move up the social and educational ladders. This upward movement is reinforced in each succeeding generation. Here again statistical evidence is scanty and based on samples of schoolchildren that are not randomly selected, and are probably in many respects atypical.

The present study provides a unique opportunity to follow the educational progress of short-sighted pupils and to look at the distribution of short sight within the population. It also allows comparisons of a number of personal characteristics and interests to be made between short-sighted pupils and those with normal vision, for example behaviour in and out of class, games ability, types of hobbies and attendance at school. Lastly, it is possible to take children before they have developed short sight and link their ability and attitudes at this earlier age with those recorded after their vision has become defective.

Short-sighted boys and girls as well as those with a variety of other defects were picked out at the medical examinations by their inability to read the lines of smaller letters on the Snellen wall chart. Long-sighted pupils however are likely to have escaped detection because they would have been able to read, at a distance, print that would have been difficult for them to decipher when held close to. The results of this test as given to members of the sample provides therefore no information on the nature of the visual defects, only on the extent of the impairment of distant vision. It is likely however that all seriously short-sighted pupils were identified.

Further information on the nature and cause of the more serious defects was obtained in the following way. A list was made of all fifteen year pupils who with their best eye and without glasses had vision of 6/12 or less, i.e. could read at no more than 6 metres away the size of print that a pupil with no visual defect could read at 12 metres or more. The names of the boys and girls on this list were sent to the appropriate Medical Officers of Health with a request for further information, including the correction prescribed.

The information obtained from the Medical Officers of Health

[154]

and from the Survey records was submitted to Dr Comer of the Royal Eye Hospital for assessment. Out of 3,775 boys and girls who were given the Snellen test at fifteen years, 2,949 had normal vision in both eyes (6/6 or better without glasses), 461 had at least one eye with good or fair, but not perfect, vision (better than 6/12), 224 were short-sighted and 141 were identified as having other defects—these included 13 who were long-sighted and some with defects that cannot be diagnosed from the information available. Full educational information, including the results of tests at eight, eleven and fifteen years, was available for 2,553 of the 2,949 children with normal vision and 171 of the 197 who were short-sighted and had had their eyes tested at seven, eleven and fifteen years. It is these two groups that are used in the following discussion.

There are no significant sex differences in the occurrence of severe short sight, but moderate short sight is more common among the girls. This is a consistent finding within each social class.

Short sight was more commonly reported for the middle than the manual working class pupils, 8 per cent in the upper middle class, 7 per cent in the lower middle and 6 and 4 per cent in the upper and lower manual working class respectively. In contrast other eye defects were equally distributed between the four social classes. In view of this and of the way in which the short-sighted boys and girls were identified, it is unlikely that the higher proportion of short-sighted children in the upper social classes can be explained by a bias in the identification of defects.

The family background of short-sighted pupils is different in many other ways from that of pupils with other defects or with normal vision. Their parents for example are more likely to have been at secondary school, while those who had elementary schooling only are more likely to have taken educational courses after leaving school; this is so for both the fathers and the mothers.* The higher educational level and aspirations of the parents of the short-sighted children is reflected in our assessments of the amount of interest they take in their children's work and progress, at both primary and secondary school. Thirty-seven per cent of the parents of children with normal vision were assessed as highly interested in their children's secondary school progress, compared with 57 per

* See Table 38.

[155]

cent of the parents of short-sighted. The fathers of short-sighted children were also more likely to visit the schools, 51 per cent did so, compared with 39 per cent of the fathers of pupils with normal vision. Lastly, more of the short-sighted pupils were provided with separate rooms for their homework—67 per cent, compared with 49 per cent of those with normal vision. In contrast there is only a small difference in the assessment of the standard of maternal care.

The high interest and aspirations of their parents are to some extent reflected in the progress of the short-sighted pupils in both primary and secondary schools. They work harder than the pupils with normal vision at each stage and are reported as being more attentive in school and more punctual. Their attendance records also are slightly more satisfactory and they are slightly less likely to cheat in class or to tell lies to get out of trouble.

In the 11+ selection examinations, the short-sighted pupils get proportionately many more selective school places than those with normal vision, and this trend is found in each social class. For example in the lower manual working class, 35 per cent of the short-sighted reach selective schools and only 13 per cent of those with no visual defect.

The considerable importance attached to the bookish interests and poor performance in games of those who are short-sighted is to some extent confirmed by the results of the present study. In answer to questions about spare time pursuits, asked when they were eleven, thirteen and fifteen years old, more of the short-sighted boys and girls reported academic hobbies and fewer that they were interested only in sport in their spare time. However their interest in sport was not greatly below that of pupils with normal vision, 34 per cent of the short-sighted boys and 14 per cent of the girls listed sport as their only hobby compared with 44 per cent of the boys and 18 per cent of the girls with normal vision. This trend was confirmed by teachers who reported that more of the pupils with normal vision were good at games. Thus the generally accepted view of the short-sighted pupil as being more interested in academic than in physical activities receives some support from this study.

Short sight often develops during the school years; 75 per cent of those who were short-sighted at fifteen had normal vision (6/6 or better) in both eyes without glasses when tested at seven and by eleven, 25 per cent were still recorded as having normal vision. Those who develop their short sight either early or late do not differ in family background or in their attitude to work. The boys and girls who are short-sighted throughout the whole of their school careers have however rather better attendance records in the primary schools and in the later years at secondary school, than either those who have normal vision or those who developed their short sight after the age of seven.

The pupils who developed their short sight after the age of seven are at fifteen years taller and heavier as a group than either those with normal vision or those who were short-sighted throughout. In view of this we looked at the age at which they reached sexual maturity and found considerable differences. Forty-seven per cent of the boys who developed short sight after eleven are in an advanced stage of maturity or fully mature at fifteen, as against 39 per cent of those who developed it between seven and eleven and 25 per cent of those who were short-sighted throughout. These figures compare with 24 per cent for the normally sighted boys. For the girls a similar though rather less consistent relationship holds, the highest proportion of early maturers being in the group which developed short sight between seven and eleven years. These differences suggest that many short-sighted boys and girls develop this defect in association with their pre-pubertal spurt in growth. It should be added however that others in cross-sectional inquiries have found no suggestion that there is a spurt of ocular growth at puberty.

The association of short sight with the early onset of puberty suggested that it might also be associated with small family size because children with few brothers and sisters reach puberty on the average at an earlier age than those with many. This is indeed so— 7 per cent of only children as compared with 4 per cent of those in families of four or more are short-sighted—but this relationship does not explain the differences in attainment, described below, between the short-sighted pupils and the rest.

We have seen that unexpectedly high proportions of the short-sighted pupils reach the selective schools (this holds for both boys and girls); the general impression that short sight and scholarship are linked is therefore upheld. A more precise description of the

[157]

academic superiority of the short-sighted pupils is however given by the results of the ability and attainment tests.

The average scores of the short-sighted pupils are higher at each age than the average scores of those with normal vision and remain so even when corrections are made for the rather higher proportion who come from the middle classes or from small families. The advantage of the short-sighted pupils is almost as marked at eight as at the succeeding ages.

At fifteen the non-verbal tests of intelligence do not distinguish clearly between the short-sighted pupils and the rest. The slight superiority of the short-sighted girls in the non-verbal test is not statistically significant; that for the boys, although significant, is smaller than for the attainment tests. It is in the verbal intelligence test, mathematics and reading that the short-sighted make substantially higher scores than those with normal vision.* The short-sighted girls make particularly high scores in the verbal intelligence test—if this test is disregarded their relative advantage over those with normal vision is only slightly greater than the boys.

A possible explanation of the higher scores of the short-sighted pupils is that the normal group includes some with long sight who, owing to this, might be handicapped in their school work. There are however two pieces of evidence refuting this suggestion. First, the removal of all pupils from the normal group for whom glasses have been prescribed leaves the average aggregate test score of the group at fifteen unaltered. Second, the 13 pupils who are known to be long-sighted—and were excluded from the normal group— have average scores at fifteen that are 0·6 points *above* the normal group.

It will be remembered that threequarters of the short-sighted pupils developed their defect after the age of seven and it is interesting to see how their test performance compares with those who were short-sighted throughout. The rather unexpected finding is that in the eight year tests those who developed short sight during their time at school, have as great an advantage over those with normal vision as they do later. This is well shown by the differences between the actual scores they make in reading and those that would have been expected on the basis of their non-verbal intelligence test

* See Table 39.

[158]

scores. At eight, eleven and fifteen the three groups of short-sighted pupils—that is those who were short-sighted throughout, those who developed it in the primary schools and those who developed it in the secondary—score considerably higher in reading than would be expected, whereas at each of the three ages, those with normal vision make lower scores.* That the pupils who develop short sight after the age of seven should have shown a superiority in reading at eight suggests that it is not short sight, as such, which directed their interests into academic channels.

Before leaving test performance and turning to other criteria of educational achievement, it is desirable to look at the extent to which the higher scores of the short-sighted can be explained by the greater proportion who came from families with few children. In each family size the short-sighted make higher mean scores in the fifteen year tests than those with normal vision. They retain this advantage even after standardizing to allow for the effects of social class within each size of family. The short-sighted boys and girls have the greatest advantage when they have no brothers or sisters.

The short-sighted pupils get more 'O' level certificates than those with normal vision and get them at a higher level. This of course follows from the fact that a relatively large proportion of them are at selective schools, but their advantage persists even when allowances are made for their differing ability. For example among those who scored between 50–59 in the tests given at fifteen, 20 per cent of the short-sighted, compared with only 10 per cent of those with normal vision, achieved a good certificate. The short-sighted stay on longer at both selective and secondary modern schools. At the secondary moderns, 25 per cent of the short-sighted pupils but only 17 per cent of those with normal vision were still at school at the end of the 1961/2 session.

The final evidence of the greater educational aspirations of the short-sighted pupils comes from their comments on higher education. Of pupils of high ability, 74 per cent of the short-sighted compared with 57 per cent of those with normal vision said they wished to continue with full-time higher education after leaving school.

As mentioned at the beginning of this chapter, there has been a certain amount of theorizing about the upward mobility of those

* See Table 40.

who are short-sighted. There is no doubt that, as a group, the short-sighted boys and girls in this study will go into occupations that have higher social and educational status than those entered by those with normal vision. Their expressed ambitions for employment suggest a greater upward social movement than is explained by their higher measured ability. At each level of ability, a higher proportion of short-sighted intend to enter the professions and a higher proportion wish to go into non-manual work rather than manual. This latter difference is particularly noticeable among those of below average ability, of whom 64 per cent of the short-sighted hope to enter clerical or other non-manual work, compared with 49 per cent of those with normal vision.

These findings will now be summarized before any explanation is offered. The short-sighted, compared with those who have normal vision, are hardworking and attentive in class, have more academic hobbies and take less interest in sport. They are successful at school and have high ambitions for further education and employment. Those who develop their short sight during the course of their school years are, on the average, taller and heavier than either the other short-sighted pupils or those with no defect, and they come into puberty earlier. In the non-verbal tests, the scores of the short-sighted are similar to those of pupils with normal vision, but in the attainment tests, and particularly in reading, the short-sighted have a considerable advantage, which extends back at least to eight years and at this early age is as evident among those who have still to become short-sighted, as among those who have already developed this defect. The parents of the short-sighted are more likely to be middle class, to have had superior education or alternatively to have tried to get it, to have small families and to take a high interest in their children's progress at school.

The educational advantage of the short-sighted is not explained by the superior social class or education of their parents, by the small families from which they come or by their earlier puberty. From their scores in the non-verbal tests, it seems that they are not markedly more intelligent than the normally sighted. Their advantage lies in superior attainment, greater application to their work and higher ambitions, and it seems likely that this is associated with the high level of support and encouragement their parents give

[160]

them in their work. The fact that their superiority in attainment is greatest in the smallest families, where it can be inferred that the influence of the parents is maximal, adds weight to this interpretation.

Short sight is largely genetically determined (Sorsby, Sheridan and Leary, 1962). It may be that, owing to the greater ease with which their eyes can accommodate to near work, there have grown up, over the generations, attitudes to education and employment that differentiate families with a persistent history of short sight from those in which short sight is rarely found. This process would be similar to that found in certain racial minorities which for centuries have excelled in certain trades or intellectual pursuits. Such an explanation would cover all the educational findings of this study including the high attainment of eight year old pupils who become short-sighted at a later age. It is supported in this study by the finding that the 53 normally sighted children of parents who are known to be short-sighted, make scores in the fifteen year tests which are 3 points higher than those to be expected after taking into account their social class, family size, housing and maternal care.

Chapter Twenty-two

Absence from School

The actual amount of time spent at school appears to have little effect, within wide limits, on the standard of work done by healthy children. For example, after eight years at school American children who enjoyed 5 months' holiday a year were as advanced in their studies as those who had been given only 4 months' holiday, and so spent the equivalent of an extra year at school. In Great Britain pupils at independent schools have approximately a month more holiday a year than those at maintained schools, and yet there is no evidence to show that they fare worse because of this; indeed many believe that the independent school pupils do better, and in an earlier chapter on these schools we reported that the pupils in some of them more than hold their own.

The previous comments however refer to pupils who are not subjected to the interference with learning which results when a child, after being away from school during term time, has to catch up with the work of the class. It has been shown that children who were often absent were less successful in their studies than their class-mates; a long run of illness may be a cause of backwardness, both by keeping a child away from school and when he returns by leaving his health impaired. It is also probable that the extent to which children fall behind in their work, after a period of absence, depends on their own character and abilities. The duller ones may be seriously hampered by minor absences, and a child who with effort has been keeping up with a class of children of average ability, may no longer be able to do so when he rejoins the class after a period of illness. Brighter children, in contrast, although perhaps behind their class-mates when they return, may well catch

[162]

up quickly if they are given special help or perhaps even this may not be necessary.

Our information on the primary school attendance of pupils in this study is very detailed;* between the ages of six and a half and ten and a half years, the teachers were asked to keep running records of the absences of the children and the reasons for them. All absences of a week or more were checked with the mothers at the next home interview, to try to verify the reason why the child was away from school. The time and effort that this method required was not thought justifiable at the secondary stage—instead the number of possible and the number of actual attendances during the pupils' thirteenth and fifteenth years were asked for. Owing to the different information on absence that we have for the primary and secondary periods, the two are considered separately when test performance and school achievement are discussed, and when discussing secondary school absences we have to consider selective and secondary modern school pupils separately.

Although reasons were given for the majority of all primary school absences, it is by no means certain that all are correct. Illness was reported as the reason for 89 per cent of the total time lost from school, but this may well be an overestimate. Minor illnesses or trivial accidents may sometimes have been used by parents or children to explain absences that were in fact to look after brothers or sisters or to join family excursions. It is only for the longer periods of absence, those lasting one week or more, that the cause can be given with confidence, thus allowing us to link sickness absence with school performance.

We first describe the types of pupil who are frequently away. In the early years at primary school, boys are rather more often away than girls, whereas in the later years there is a slight excess of absence among the girls. This excess for the girls also holds at secondary school, and is partly explained by an increase in absences among girls who have started their periods. It is particularly middle class girls at secondary modern schools who lose much time after reaching puberty; whereas manual working class girls are less affected for this reason.

There are only small social class differences in the amount of time

* For a discussion of primary school absences see Douglas and Ross (1965).

lost in the primary schools. During the early years middle class boys and girls are rather more often absent than the manual working class, but later the manual working class pupils are more likely to be away. In the selective schools overall social class differences in absence are also small, but this is partly because the patterns of the boys and girls are different. Manual working class boys are more likely than middle class boys to lose time from the selective schools, whereas manual working class girls at selective schools are rather better attenders than middle class girls. In contrast the manual working class girls at secondary schools have the worst absence records being twice as likely as their selective school contemporaries to be often absent. The middle class boys and girls at secondary modern schools are rather more likely to be absent than those at selective schools, but manual working class boys show an equally high level of absence whether they are at selective or non-selective schools.

School attendance is more satisfactory at both primary and secondary schools for those boys and girls whose parents take an active interest in their school work, but this effect is more evident at the older age, especially among the secondary modern school pupils.

At each stage of their school careers, the poor attenders are less favourably regarded by their teachers than those who are seldom away. Except for the middle class pupils at selective schools, they are relatively often assessed as poor workers throughout. They are also picked out by their teachers as showing a number of signs of disturbed behaviour.

It is the general impression among those who work in education that the absence record of a class of school children tells a great deal about the qualities of the teacher. In the present study, it is found that the schools favourably assessed for staffing, for gaining 11 + places at grammar schools or for retaining their pupils after the age of fifteen are also those in which absence rates are low.

Absences are not equally likely throughout the primary school years. Between the ages of six and a half and seven and a half an average of 4 weeks of schooling was lost, whereas in each of the following three years this dropped to $2\frac{1}{2}$ weeks. No doubt, if absence records had been available for the year school was started, more time would have been lost than the 4 weeks reported for the second

[164]

year at school, for illness spreads quickly among young children when they are new to school and encountering a greater load of infection than they have met previously.

The information on absences in the primary schools has been summarized in three ways: first, the total amount of time lost from school; second, the number of episodes of absence; and third, the amount of time lost through absences of more than one week which are known to be due to illness. Of these the number of episodes of absence shows the closest association with school progress and it seems that a succession of minor breaks of schooling is more damaging than a few major breaks, even when the total time lost is similar. For example in the lower manual working class, the eleven year test scores of pupils who have lost most time from school are, on the average, 3·2 points below those who have lost least, whereas if the same comparisons are made using episodes lost rather than weeks, the difference is 5·2 points. In this comparison, the extreme groups of pupils in each instance are those falling into the top or bottom 16 per cent of the absence distribution for the whole sample.

The following observations on primary school absences are therefore based on the number of episodes, or spells, of absence and not on the actual time lost. These episodes of absence have been grouped so as to give the pattern of absences over the four years for which records are available.

The effects of absence on school performance depend both on the family and on the school. The middle class boys and girls who have been absent frequently throughout their primary school years are little handicapped, and in the primary schools which have good past records for getting grammar school places, frequent absences also appear to have little effect. It is in the lower manual working class families, particularly when the pupils are attending schools which have a relatively poor past record of academic success, that frequent episodes of absence are associated with poor and deteriorating test performance. These boys and girls have lower scores for the attainment than the non-verbal tests, and their under-achievement is most evident in arithmetic.

The pupils frequently absent before the age of eight and a half, but not in the following two years, are not handicapped in their test

[165]

scores. Indeed in the upper middle and to a lesser extent in the lower middle and upper manual working classes, those who were absent in the early years at primary school show a greater improvement in test score than those who were good attenders throughout; this might be explained by a temporary depression at eight years. It is of considerable interest that the lower manual working class pupils, and those who attend primary schools with poor academic records, do not catch up in this way after heavy absences between the ages of six and a half and eight and a half. Pupils from all except upper middle class homes who were consistently absent throughout the four year period or who, after being good attenders in the first two years, lost much time from school later, are considerably affected. They deteriorate in test score between eight and eleven and moreover, get fewer grammar school places in the 11+ selection examinations than would be expected from their ability as measured by tests at that age. Poor attendance has a greater effect on 11+ selection among manual working class pupils than among middle class, and it is particularly the boys and girls whose ability is at the borderline level of entry to grammar school who are affected.

So far we have considered episodes of absence in the primary schools irrespective of their cause. As already mentioned absences of a week or more were checked at home visits and we are reasonably confident that we have, in this way, isolated those attributable to illness—though of course they exclude the short spells of illness that may keep a child away for a few days. The amount of time lost through illness measured in this way is very similar in each social class, and there are no significant differences between the boys and girls. There is no evidence that those who have lost six weeks or less from primary school through major episodes of illness have suffered for it, but those who have lost more than six weeks make lower scores in the tests at each age. The effects of illness absence are however limited to the manual working class pupils who are little down in the non-verbal tests whereas the verbal and two attainment scores are considerably depressed, and this depression persists at the age of fifteen.

In the secondary schools, the pupils are divided into three groups according to the amount of time lost in their thirteenth and fifteenth years. The same division is used for the selective and secondary

[166]

modern school pupils, and it divides all the pupils roughly into thirds according to their attendance records. In the selective schools, the test performance of the middle class boys and girls is little affected by the amount of time lost from school, whereas the scores of the manual working class pupils who have consistently been away are down in all tests—particularly in mathematics.* The secondary modern school pupils who have been frequently absent show a similar pattern in each social class, namely lower scores in all the fifteen year old tests. These pupils are particularly down in mathematics and verbal intelligence.

The manual working class pupils who have frequently been away from their selective schools also do less well than expected in the 'O' level examinations, even after account has been taken of their lower test scores. In contrast the middle class pupils at selective schools who have been frequently absent do as well in the General Certificate as those who have been good attenders.

Finally a history of frequent absence from selective school is associated with early leaving for the middle class as well as the manual working pupils, and this also holds for all pupils in the secondary modern schools.†

The less detailed information on secondary schools absence therefore in its main outlines confirms the earlier findings about primary school absence: the effects depend not only on the amount of time lost, but also on the family and school. Some of these effects no doubt reflect the association between poor attendance and lack of parental interest and encouragement, though the relationship between absence through illness in the primary school and poor attainment suggests that this is no more than a partial explanation. When home conditions are good and when the schools have high academic standards, pupils can miss a considerable amount of class work and yet in the long run not fall behind in attainment, or in examination performance. When however either or both these favourable influences are wanting, absence, from whatever cause, is likely to be associated with a deterioration in performance.

The reasons for absence from the secondary schools are not known, so it is impossible to contrast the effects of absence from

---

* See Table 41.
† See Table 42.

[167]

different causes. A number of pupils were however admitted to hospitals, and some indication of the effects of serious illness may be obtained from their histories. Fifty-two per cent of the boys and 44 per cent of the girls had been inpatients on one or more occasions by the time they had reached the age of fifteen, but only 27 of the boys and 24 of the girls in the educational sample had spent more than three weeks in hospital during their secondary school years. Another 135, who had had no hospital admissions, or admissions for only short periods between the ages of eleven and fifteen, had spent more than three weeks in hospital during their primary school years, and a further 159 had had similar long spells of hospital admissions in their pre-school years, but not later. These three groups may be compared with those who had no hospital admissions at all and with those who had no long spells of admission. Social class differences in the proportion of boys and girls admitted to hospital in each of these groups are small and insignificant, but more middle than manual working class boys were admitted to hospital as short stay patients. For the girls there is no social class difference.

There is no evidence to suggest that admission to hospital during the school years influences the ability and attainment of pupils, their General Certificate results or the age at which they leave school. In the sample as a whole, and in each social group separately, those who have lost more than three weeks through hospital admissions during their secondary school years do as well as those who have not been to hospital at all; and the same holds for those who have lost a similar amount of time through hospital admission in their primary school years.

Hospital admissions, without added information on the types of illness, and the disabilities and handicaps associated with them, form too blunt a probe to be used to assess the influence of illness on school performance. It is evident however that the length of stay in hospital alone within wide limits is unlikely to be a serious handicap to the school progress of pupils from any social class, probably because adequate steps are taken to help them with their work. The wider problem of the effect of illness is discussed in the following chapter.

[168]

Chapter Twenty-three

A Heavy Load of Illness*

The illnesses of childhood may, for general purposes, be divided into those that are 'minor-episodic' and those that are 'major-chronic'. The first group includes disorders which are, for the most part, of short duration—such as episodic conditions of the new born, common infectious diseases, and minor accidents. The second group includes disorders of rather longer duration and usually of more serious import. This chapter discusses the educational progress and attainment only of those pupils in the major-chronic illness category, for it is reasonable to suppose that these disorders are the ones which are likely to interfere most with school work.

We have seen that the effects of absence vary with school and family background. However inability to attend school regularly is only one of the educational problems associated with major-chronic conditions. Those conditions with marked constitutional components may have a direct influence on children's stamina or on their ability to concentrate. Conditions involving the central nervous system, even if they do not produce mental subnormality, may be associated with specific learning difficulties. Some pupils with serious defects may become discouraged about their academic or occupational prospects and see little point in applying themselves to their school work, whereas others may increase their efforts in order to compensate for their disabilities.

Perhaps the most important way in which a major-chronic illness may affect performance is by influencing the pupil's perception of himself, and hence his behaviour. From clinical observations it

* Based on an interim report by Dr Barry Pless.

[169]

seems that many children with these disorders are affected emotion-ally—some become depressed, dependent and neurotic, while others show signs of aggression and assume an air of defiance and in-dependence in an attempt to deny to themselves and others the fact that they are in some respects disabled. In this connection the nature of the family unit and the kind of support it provides for the child may be of crucial importance.

The school progress of the boys and girls who suffered from major chronic disorders will now be discussed. Included in this group is any child who, owing to illness, has for a minimum of three months in any year been prevented from carrying out activities appropriate to his age and sex, or been able to carry them out only with difficulty or distress. An additional group is formed by those whose illness kept them in hospital for one month or more in any year, even if they were not restricted in their activities on discharge. Detailed scrutiny of the boys and girls in the Survey provided a group of 535 with conditions which, in severity or duration, satisfied these criteria. They included congenital abnormalities, heart and lung disorders, poor vision, defective hearing, speech disorders, epilepsy and diseases affecting the limbs and muscles. No child was included solely on the grounds of emotional illness or mental sub-normality, on the other hand no child was excluded if these condi-tions were associated with physical disorder. Of the 524 surviving children with a heavy load of illness (approximately 12 per cent of those at risk), 405 are included in the educational sample and of these 14 were at special schools.*

Compared with the rest of the population the group of sick† children contains a slight excess of boys and those from large families; in addition, rather more of their mothers described them-selves as being in poor health, or as having chronic illnesses. There is no suggestion that proportionately more of the sick children come from the poorer social classes.

There is a number of reasons for predicting that the sick children will, as a group, be academically retarded. They are much more

---

* Of the 14 pupils, 6 were at schools for the educationally subnormal, 5 for the delicate and physically handicapped, 2 were partially sighted, 1 epileptic.

† To avoid cumbersome phrases the words 'sick' and 'healthy' are used to describe the two groups, those with a heavy load of illness and the rest.

frequently away from both the primary and the secondary schools than the healthy children and are more likely than the rest of the pupils to be rated by the primary school teachers as poor workers. In the secondary schools they are picked out both for their lack of application to work and their troublesome behaviour. In the secondary schools, there is a slight excess of truancy among the sick pupils though this difference is small and not statistically significant. Their teachers rated relatively more of them at both thirteen and fifteen as being very nervous in their general behaviour or as being both nervous and aggressive, and the number of sick children with symptoms at fifteen is high. The sick pupils do not however show themselves on the self-rating inventory as anxious or neurotic. The only assessment that is favourable to them, and this is not statistically significant, is parents' interest. The parents appear to take slightly more interest in their school work than do the parents of those who have not had illnesses classed as major-chronic.

From the amount of time lost from schools, from their failure to work hard and from their troublesome behaviour in class, it would seem that the educational progress of the sick pupils would be retarded compared with the healthy. The adverse ratings of behaviour made by the teachers and the mothers would also lead one to expect relatively poor test performance and early leaving. Further the fact that a higher proportion of the sick children have many brothers and sisters would seem to predict poorer academic performance.

The average aggregate test score of the sick pupils is below that of the healthy, and this is so even after allowing for differences in family size, housing, and standards of maternal care. For the whole group of sick children the depression in test score though statistically significant is relatively small, and is moreover similar at each age. There is no suggestion of a deterioration in performance over the school years, which would be expected if the illness itself, or the absence associated with it, were interfering with learning. When however the sick pupils are sub-divided by the severity of their condition the following pattern emerges. Those who are only mildly affected—rather more than half of the group (237)—show no deficit in test score at fifteen; those who are moderately affected

[171]

(133) are 1·7 points below the expected score at fifteen; and those who are severely affected (37) are 5·0 points below. It is only in the last group that there is a deterioration in test performance between eight and fifteen. At eight the severely affected have scores that are similar to the mildly affected, at fifteen they are 4·6 points below.

The average reading scores of the severely sick pupils are also low. When the reading scores expected from the non-verbal test results are compared with the actual scores, it is found that at eight the severely sick pupils are on average 2 points below the level expected, whereas at fifteen they are nearly 5 points below. For neither the mild nor the moderately affected pupils is there a significant degree of under-achievement in reading at any age.

As expected from their test performance at eleven, rather fewer of the sick children reach the selective schools. There is however no evidence that they are handicapped over and above this. Even without taking account of the slightly higher proportion at secondary modern schools, the leaving ages of sick pupils are similar to the rest, while when comparisons are made between pupils of similar ability, they are indeed more likely to stay on at school and more likely to wish to enter higher education after leaving school.

A similar impression of good progress and attainment is given by the results of the 'O' level examinations of the sick pupils. At each level of ability, those with a heavy load of illness are more likely to get certificates than the healthy and at the borderline level of ability slightly more of them get good certificates. This is so whether comparisons are made between pupils at selective schools or between pupils at non-selective. It is however in the latter that the sick group appear to have the greatest academic advantage. It seemed possible that the advantage of the sick pupils came from including those with severe short sight, but the exclusion of these few boys and girls still left the sick pupils with better 'O' level results, and longer school life than the healthy.

When the total group of sick children is divided up by the severity of their conditions, it is found that even the seriously disabled, who include three at special schools for the educationally subnormal, overall have a slight advantage compared with the well. Indeed if they are further sub-divided by the duration of the condition those with long lasting disabilities have a slight, though statistically insignificant,

[172]

advantage in the 'O' level examinations over those whose disabilities are only temporary.

By considering the group of major-chronic disorders as a whole, regardless of the more detailed characteristics of each condition, it was hoped to show that the pupils with a heavy load of illness had common educational problems, as well as problems which were related to their individual illnesses. It turns out that in spite of much absence, poor work and behaviour assessments both in and out of class, it is only the small group of 37 severely affected who appear to be under-achieving in attainment tests, and even they are favourably placed as regards both age of leaving school and 'O' level certificates. A possible explanation would be that pupils with a heavy load of illness are compensating in their work for disabilities that prevent many from taking a full part in out-of-class activities. The favourable performance of these pupils in non-selective schools could be accounted for by the lower level of academic competition which they encounter. This would make it easier for them, if they were indeed compensating for their physical disabilities with hard work, to outstrip their class-mates. The teachers' assessments of class behaviour however give no support to this view.

It seems then that the school work of pupils with a heavy load of illness does not suffer if they are kept within the main stream of school life; these pupils may moreover gain social advantages from avoiding the relative isolation that so often accompanies education in special schools. To meet the educational needs of pupils with asthma, heart disease, epilepsy, etc. in normal schools may present formidable tasks for their teachers—but the results of this study show that the additional effort is well justified.

Part V

Summing Up

Chapter Twenty-four

Influence of Home and School

The additional information gathered during the secondary school years, reiterates and underlines the importance of the home in shaping educational attitudes and attainment. This book provides many indications that the influences are greatest at two periods; first during the pre-school years, and second at the end of the compulsory school period when many pupils leave, including a number of very able boys and girls.

The importance of the home influences in the pre-school years was obscured in *The Home and the School* by the fact that there appeared to be an increasing social class gap in test performance, between the ages of eight and eleven. This was interpreted as indicating the growing influence of the environment on the measured ability and attainment of primary school children, an interpretation that, with the additional information available, must now be modified. The divergence of the intelligence test results seems to be a temporary artifact of the stresses of secondary selection rather than the result of real changes in the ability of the boys and girls (see Chapter III). The gap between the social classes in non-verbal test scores is no greater at fifteen than at eight, and while there is a slightly greater gap between them in attainment at fifteen, this is largely owing to the high scores made by the upper middle class boys and girls. It seems then that once the pupils are grouped by their family background, the main characteristics of their test performance are determined by the age of eight and possibly earlier, though how much earlier we do not know.

We attribute many of the major differences in performance to environmental influences acting in the pre-school years. Many

[177]

factors appear to have exerted their main influence on measured ability by the time children leave the infant schools. For example the low attainment of pupils in the manual working classes (Chapter III), or in large families where there are many brothers and sisters near to them in age (Chapter XVII), or who have many signs or symptoms of disturbed behaviour (Chapter XV), is present at eight and changes little in the subsequent seven years. And the same holds for the superior attainment of elder boys in two-child families and of both boys and girls with medium birth intervals of 2–4 years (Chapter XVIII).

The observation that short-sighted pupils are superior in attainment to those with good vision allows us to give a rough estimate of the relative importance of home influences on test performance, before and after the age of eight, since it seems that their superior attainment is linked to the high level of interest shown by their parents rather than to their visual defect (Chapter XXI). By the age of eight the short-sighted have acquired approximately threequarters of their total advantage—they are then roughly 3 points of test score ahead of those with good vision, while at fifteen their lead is increased by only one further point. It is also interesting to note that the greatest advantage in attainment of the short-sighted over the normally sighted is among only children—in other words those whose contacts with adults are closest. It is necessary to know a great deal more about the process of transmission of attitudes and knowledge from one generation to the next, before it is possible to suggest how to replace or augment the stimulation that many children, from their family circumstances, appear to lack.*

That pupils are influenced during their years at school by their home circumstances is also clear from this study. These influences undoubtedly shape attitudes to school and learning; they are more apparent in leaving age, in the results of the General Certificate of Education examinations and in the wish to enter higher education, than they are in the test score results. This stems in part from the parents' choice of school. Some parents are able and anxious to pick out the better schools and, particularly in the middle class,

* Children from large families may of course benefit in other ways through social contacts with children near them in age. This again is something that needs investigation.

are more prepared and better able to move to areas where good schools are known to be available. Parental attitudes may also perhaps explain some of the relative deterioration of girls in the tests given at fifteen, although as we have seen in Chapter X much depends on the type of school they attend; in co-educational schools for example the girls have at fifteen a similar level of achievement to the boys.

In the primary schools, deficiencies of interest and ambition on the part of the parents are, to some extent, offset by good teaching. The influence of the primary schools extends also to the secondary schools and affects later development and progress. For example the persisting influence of streaming in the primary schools is illustrated by the secondary school histories of children who, as reported in *The Home and the School,* had been placed in one or other stream of two-stream schools, allocation being based on estimates of ability made before eight. In the later years at primary school, the pupils in the top stream improved in measured ability, whereas those in the bottom deteriorated. They conformed much more closely than would have been expected to early estimates based on relatively crude measurements of ability. The lower stream pupils who, with one exception, went to secondary modern schools, did not show any further fall in measured ability and attainment compared with those who had been in the upper stream. Indeed the manual working class boys who had been in the bottom stream improved their test performance between eleven and fifteen years, particularly in reading and mathematics. At each level of ability at fifteen however the pupils who had been in the lower stream when they were in their primary schools, left earlier than those from the top. There is conflicting evidence here; on the one hand the depression of test performance for those in the lower stream does not persist at fifteen, on the other hand they leave the secondary modern schools early. How far is this to be explained by the expectations of academic failure that were fostered in the primary schools?

There is evidence that the social background of the primary schools has a persisting influence on secondary school performance. Some primary schools recruit their pupils mainly from families of clerks and other middle class workers, including those in the professions, while others recruit them predominantly from the manual working class. Between the ages of eight and eleven pupils in those primary schools which enrolled their pupils predominantly from the manual working class fell behind the rest in their test performance and at each level of ability were less likely to be allocated to grammar schools. These same pupils are likely to leave early and so seldom sit the General Certificate examinations. At secondary modern schools, they are only two-thirds as likely to stay to the end of the 1961/2 session as are those of similar measured ability coming from primary schools with a largely non-manual intake. If they go to grammar schools, they are also at a similar disadvantage. The influence of the primary school is particularly strong for the manual working class child; if he has been to a primary school that is predominantly middle class, he is more likely to succeed at secondary school, than if he had been to a primary school recruiting its pupils mainly from the manual working class.

These observations suggest that children acquire, early in their years at school, attitudes to learning that are related to later success or failure. The primary school influence is most clearly seen among the secondary modern school pupils, perhaps because they have a less positive attitude towards education than those at grammar school and so are less able to alter the expectations and habitual attitudes that were acquired at a younger age.

Social inequalities in selection to the secondary schools are most apparent for those at the borderline level of ability—the boys and girls of high ability having similar chances of securing grammar school places, whatever their home circumstances. It was to be expected that nearly all the pupils of high ability, some of whom have struggled against considerable difficulties to reach the grammar schools, would be supported by the academic traditions of their schools and stay on at least to enter the sixth form. This is not so and it is disturbing to find that so many leave early and fail to sit the General Certificate examinations.

In order to summarize the extent to which educational progress is influenced by the home and the school we have related the length of school life of the lower manual working class pupils of borderline ability and above to a large number of factors in their homes and schools. The lower manual working class was chosen

[180]

as showing the greatest waste of talent, and the borderline and high ability pupils were chosen as comprising the majority of those in this social class who would be likely to benefit from sixth form work and who, if they came from middle class homes, would mostly do so. We felt that, with the available educational criteria, it was more realistic to study waste among those of high ability than failure to provide opportunities for those of lower ability. At a later stage, when success can be judged in a wider setting, we hope to extend this comparison to those of average ability and below.

The lower manual working class groups of both high and borderline ability show on the whole the expected relationships between the length of school life and the various factors we have discussed throughout this book. Those who were picked out by their teachers as being nervous or aggressive are more likely than the rest to leave early, so also are those who were reported at fifteen to have one or more symptoms of disturbed behaviour, to be inattentive, troublesome, or often away in either their primary or secondary schools, or to be delinquent or truant. Pupils aiming at professional as opposed to other employment after leaving school are more likely to stay on, especially in the group of borderline ability.

By definition all the parents of these lower manual working class boys and girls had left school themselves before reaching the age of 15, but the pupils whose parents had attempted to obtain some further education after entering employment are nearly twice as likely to stay on as the rest. This applies equally to the fathers' and the mothers' education. Poor health of either parent is related to early leaving in the high ability group, and in both groups those whose mothers have high neuroticism scores on the Maudsley Personality Inventory are more likely to leave early. A high level of parental interest, high employment ambitions for the child and a good record of visits to the school on the part of the father are all associated with longer school life.

Clear evidence of the importance of the primary school is found for those of high ability. In this group the average age of leaving school is later for those who were at primary schools in urban areas, with good amenities, with good past records of 11 + success or with a predominantly middle class intake of pupils. None of these primary

[181]

school characteristics was however related to the length of school life in the borderline group; this is unexpected for in *The Home and the School* it was shown that the relationship between the primary schools' past record of 11+ successes and the pupils' chance of reaching grammar school was particularly high for pupils at this level of ability.

At the secondary schools the position is complicated by the need to split the sample into selective and secondary modern school pupils. The 157 lower manual working class boys and girls of high or borderline ability attending selective schools are not sufficiently differentiated in respect of the size, amenities, or staffing of their schools, to make a detailed study profitable.

There are much larger differences in the characteristics of the schools attended by the 176 secondary modern school pupils, and these we now relate to age of leaving. Early leaving is more frequent in secondary modern schools that have less than 600 pupils, are built on poor or noisy sites, have a majority of children of unskilled manual workers, have a poor past record of retaining their pupils beyond the statutory leaving age, have few graduates on the staff and have a high ratio of pupils to teachers.*

We now turn from a general description of the individual factors influencing the age of leaving secondary modern schools to an assessment of the relative importance of the school and the home on the length of school life of these lower manual working class pupils. Owing to the many factors involved, it was necessary to construct two simple scales, one assessing parental attitudes and the other assessing the characteristics of the secondary modern schools. These are more inclusive than our previous measures of 'parental interest' and 'school type'. (See Chapters III and VII.)

We have grouped the parents of these able lower manual working class boys and girls according to the following criteria.

(a) One point was given if either the father or the mother or both had sought further education after leaving school;

(b) One point was given if the father had visited the school to discuss his child's progress on more than two occasions and/or the parents were assessed by the teachers as taking a high level of interest in their children's work;

* See Table 43.

[182]

(c) One point was given if the mothers wished their children to follow a full-time educational course on leaving school and/or to enter a profession.

The lowest score on this scale is 0, showing the least parental involvement, the highest is 3; in practice however so few scored 3 that we grouped them with those who scored 2. Combining the high ability and borderline pupils 33 per cent of the parents of those at secondary modern schools scored 0, 51 per cent scored 1 and 15 per cent were in the highest group, that is to say scored 2 or 3.

The secondary modern schools were also grouped into three in the following way, their scored running from 0 to 2.

(a) One point was given for either good school amenities or more than 600 pupils, or both of these;

(b) One point was given for 20 per cent or more graduate staff or for a pupil/teacher ratio of less than 19, or both of these.

Twenty-eight per cent of the lower manual working class pupils under consideration were at secondary modern schools in which there were deficiencies of both staffing and amenities (i.e. a score of 0), 39 per cent were in schools scoring intermediately and 33 per cent were in schools both with good amenities and a satisfactory staff.

By relating the two scales—parents attitudes and school characteristics—9 groups of boys and 9 groups of girls in secondary modern schools are obtained.

There is a clear relationship between the parental and school scores, the favourably assessed parents are also the most likely to send their children to the favourably assessed schools. Of the boys and girls whose parents scored 0 on the attitude scale, 34 per cent were at the least satisfactory secondary modern schools, whereas of those whose parents scored the highest, only 22 per cent were at these schools. One cannot say of course how much of this difference represents choice on the part of the parents and how much the impact of the schools, both primary and secondary, on the attitudes of the parents and on their expectations.

In order to remove the overlapping effects of sex, parental interest and school characteristics on the proportions of pupils staying to the end of the 1961/2 session, we have used an analysis of variance

[183]

method involving the fitting of constants. The results of this analysis (see Diagram VI) show that there are no significant differences between the proportions of boys and girls staying to the end of the 1961/2 session, 32 per cent of the boys and 33 per cent of the girls.

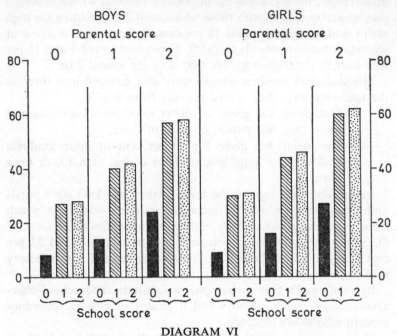

DIAGRAM VI

The percentages staying at least to the end of 1961/2 session related to parental attitudes and school characteristics—lower manual working class pupils of borderline ability and above, at secondary modern schools.

There is however a sharp rise in the proportion of pupils staying on as the parental score increases—for example of those with parents who have a score of 0, 23 per cent stayed on, of those with a score of 1, 35 per cent and of those with a score of 2 or 3, 50 per cent. There is also a similar gradient when we look at the school scales, though here it is only the schools with a score of 0 who differ from the rest; in these schools only 15 per cent stay on to the end of the 1961/2 session, this compares with 40 per cent of the pupils in schools with a score of 1 and 42 per cent in schools with a score of

2. It is only when schools are adversely assessed on both criteria that the leaving pattern is affected.

The Plowden Committee suggested that priority areas should be established in which additional money should be earmarked to raise the standards of the local primary schools—both buildings and teaching. It seems that there is also a need for similar priority areas at the secondary stage. Twenty-eight per cent of these lower manual working class pupils of relatively high ability were in secondary modern schools that lacked amenities and had serious staffing problems and the evidence is that these pupils left the earliest, even if the level of their parents' interest was high. For example if their parents' interest and aspirations were high only 25 per cent of these boys and girls stayed to the end of the 1961/2 session in the worst schools, compared with 60 per cent in the best. Among those with the least favourably assessed parents 9 per cent and 30 per cent stayed on in the poor and well equipped schools respectively. It seems that high parental interest alone is insufficient to counter the deficiences of the schools. The following quotation from the Plowden Report is as relevant to the secondary as to the primary schools: 'It should not be assumed that even the ablest children can surmount every handicap, they may suffer as much as any from adverse conditions.'

The conclusions of this chapter are that, in the selective secondary system which existed between 1957 and 1962, social inequalities in educational opportunity could have been greatly reduced by raising the standards of many of the existing schools, by increasing the provision of grammar, direct grant and technical schools and by removing local inequalities in the provision of selective places—these inequalities are largely historic and bear little relation to the ability of the pupils living in each area. A general improvement in the staffing and amenities of many of the schools and the elimination of local discrepancies are, and will be, no less necessary in the comprehensive system of secondary education which is now evolving: it requires and will require an equally great investment and direction of both capital and staff.

Chapter Twenty-five

Summary of Main Conclusions

These brief comments are not meant to provide a summary of all the findings of this book. They select those observations which seem to us to be educationally important, or unexpected in the sense that they conflict with established views. In presenting them, we hope that the reader will trace back the chapter references so that he will be in a better position to appreciate the weight of evidence on which they are based.

The National Survey

1. This book is a sequel to *The Home and the School*, it describes the educational progress of the same group of boys and girls during their first five years at secondary school.

2. Losses have been small and the group is still a representative sample of all those born in Great Britain in 1946. The tests and questionnaires they have filled in for this inquiry, and the special attention that may have been given them by their parents and teachers, have not in any detectable way influenced their school progress. (Chapter II.)

Educational Opportunity

3. The social class differences in educational opportunity which were considerable at the primary school stage have increased at the secondary and extend now even to pupils of high ability. Thus nearly half the lower manual working class pupils of high ability have left school before they are sixteen and a half years. (Chapter IV.)

4. Early leaving and low job aspirations make it probable that as many as 5 per cent of the next generation of manual workers

will be recruited from pupils who, in other circumstances, might have qualified for administrative or professional occupations. (Chapter XII.)

5. The manual working class pupils, compared with those of the middle class, are least handicapped when they are in the best staffed and best equipped schools (Chapters VI and VII) and in those areas of the country which have the largest proportion of selective school places. (Chapter XI.)

6. An analysis of the length of school life among the lower manual working class pupils of borderline ability and above shows that both parental interest and school staffing and equipment are associated with age of leaving. These two factors are of course highly correlated, but neither adequately compensates for the deficiency of the other—the interest of the parents alone is insufficient to counter the deficiences of the schools. (Chapter XXIV.)

Independent Schools

7. The pupils at the boys' public schools, once their ability and the circumstances of their families are taken into account, are no more successful, as judged by 'O' level results and age of leaving up to sixteen and a half years, than grammar school pupils. The pupils at other independent schools (i.e. those outside the Headmasters' Conference) are considerably less successful. (Chapter VIII.)

8. The pupils at independent girls' schools are considerably less successful than those at grammar schools. They leave earlier and have less good 'O' level results, whether the schools are members of the Headmistresses' Association or not. (Chapter VIII.)

Educational Progress of Boys and Girls

9. The test scores of the girls, on the average, fall below those of the boys between the ages of eleven and fifteen—with the one exception of the verbal intelligence test. Their disadvantage in each social class is greatest in mathematics. Girls on the whole are less likely to get good 'O' level certificates than boys but once allowances are made for their lower measured ability at fifteen, their 'O' level results are no worse than the boys' and indeed at lower levels of ability are rather better. (Chapter V.)

[187]

10. In co-educational schools, the average fifteen year test performance of the boys and girls is similar and even in mathematics the girls are not significantly below the boys. At co-educational grammar schools the early maturing girls stay on as long or longer than late maturing girls, whereas at single sex grammar schools they leave earlier. (Chapter X.)

Education North and South of the Border

11. Scottish pupils at each age make lower scores in non-verbal tests than the English and Welsh. In reading, the Scots are ahead at eight but not later, and in arithmetic and mathematics they have a persisting lead over those south of the border. Rather more Scottish pupils leave at the earliest opportunity but the proportions staying on to the beginning of the 1962/3 session and the proportions gaining 'O' level passes are similar in the two countries. A higher percentage of Scottish than English and Welsh boys expect to enter higher education. (Chapter XI.)

Parental Influences

12. The attitudes of the parents to the education of their children changed little over the period covered by this study. (Chapter XII.)

13. Parents of widely different ages have similar educational aspirations for their children and it seems that they adopt current attitudes towards education rather than carry forward those of their own generation. (Chapter XII.)

14. The interest and encouragement that parents give their children is closely linked to their own educational history. Any attempt that the parents made to secure for themselves education beyond the elementary school level, even if this was not successfully completed, is associated with higher aspirations for their own children's educational success. (Chapter XII.)

15. Insecurity in a family, whether from father's absence, unemployment, illness or death, is associated with poorer performance at school and early leaving. It is prolonged insecurity that seems to be important; the sudden death of a father, whether early or late in the life of his child, has no apparent effect on school work. (Chapter XIII.)

[188]

Troublesome or Disturbed Pupils

16. Pupils who are described by their teachers as troublesome or inattentive in class show a deterioration in test performance, particularly in attainment, during their years at school. Compared with pupils of similar ability at the age of fifteen, the troublesome or inattentive get fewer 'O' levels than expected and are more likely to leave early than those who are favourably assessed. (Chapter XIV.)

17. Pupils who show few signs and symptoms of disturbed behaviour out of class make, on the average, higher scores in the tests of ability and attainment, do better in the General Certificate of Education examinations and stay on longer at school; in contrast those with many signs and symptoms make lower scores, get fewer 'O' levels and leave earlier. These differences at fifteen are similar to those found at eight and eleven years: pupils with many signs and symptoms are persistently poor scholars, throughout their school careers, not merely at the older ages. There is however a small group who are picked out by their teachers as nervous or aggressive, by their mothers as having many habit symptoms, and who in addition rate themselves as anxious or neurotic. This small group deteriorates in test performance during the school years, and presents a serious educational problem. (Chapter XV.)

18. The test performances of the delinquent boys and those who have many signs or symptoms of disturbed behaviour have much in common. Both groups make low scores at each age tested, though there is little evidence of a progressive deterioration between eleven and fifteen, in spite of the fact that many of the delinquents play truant and, on average, lose much time from school through absence. (Chapter XVI.)

19. The risks of delinquency are higher than expected when the family is broken by divorce or separation but not when the home background is insecure for other reasons. But threequarters of the sons of divorced and separated parents do not become delinquent. (Chapter XVI.)

Family Structure

20. Children from large families make low scores in all attainment tests at all ages. There is however no evidence of an increasing

[189]

educational handicap at secondary school, indeed in the manual working class there is rather less difference in the attainment of children from large and small families at fifteen, than there was when they were first tested at eight. (Chapter XVII.)

21. The more young children there are in the family when a child is learning to talk the lower his score in the eight year old vocabulary test. This early deficiency in the understanding of words is not made up later. (Chapter XVII.)

22. Pupils from large families leave school earlier than expected at each level of measured ability. Financial reasons alone are insufficient to explain this for the youngest in large families also leave early, even though there are likely to be fewer calls on the family income than when their elder brothers and sisters were the same age. (Chapter XVII.)

23. First-born boys in families of 2 or 3 make higher scores in the attainment tests and are academically more successful and more aspiring than their younger brothers and sisters. They are also superior in attainment to only children. For the girls this difference is not found. (Chapter XVIII.)

24. Pupils from two-child families with birth intervals of 2 to 4 years make higher scores in all tests than those with either shorter or longer intervals, they get superior 'O' level results and leave school later. This holds for both older and younger boys and girls: the advantage of those with 2 to 4 year intervals being as great at eight as later. (Chapter XVIII.)

Puberty

25. The average age of reaching puberty for both the boys and girls is similar in each social class. (Chapter XIX.)

26. The early maturing boys and girls make higher scores in the attainment tests at eight years as well as later, get better 'O' levels and stay on longer at school, than the later maturers. Their advantage however appears to be largely explained by the fact that proportionately more children from small families come into puberty early. It seems that stage of puberty need not be taken into account when selecting or allocating pupils to streams or schools. (Chapter XIX.)

27. There is a relatively large fall out of early maturing manual

working class boys and girls from selective schools after the 'O' level examinations. (Chapter XIX.)

Short Sight

28. The short-sighted pupils have, at each age tested, superior attainment scores to those with normal vision; their non-verbal intelligence scores are however similar. They have higher job aspirations at each level of ability than those with normal vision and more academic hobbies. (Chapter XXI.)

29. Some two-thirds of the short-sighted pupils developed their defect during the school years; they were as much superior in attainment before they became short-sighted as later. This fact, taken in conjunction with the observation that the parents of the short-sighted had had superior educational ambitions for themselves and were also more ambitious for their children, suggests that owing to the greater ease with which short-sighted persons can accomodate to near work, there have grown up over the generations attitudes to education and employment that differentiate families with a history of persistent short sight from those where short sight is rarely found. (Chapter XXI.)

Absence and Illness

30. Absence from school at either the primary or secondary stage, is associated with poor performance in tests, with early leaving and few 'O' level passes. This does not hold however for all pupils—those from middle class families or who are attending primary schools with good academic records do not fall behind in test score, even if they have been absent fairly frequently. It is the lower manual working class pupils, especially if they are attending the academically poorer schools, whose work suffers as a result of absence. (Chapter XXII.)

31. Even severe illness in childhood has little effect on school progress. Among those with a heavy load of illness, there is a slight depression of test performance, but General Certificate results and age of leaving are unaffected. (Chapter XXIII.)

[191]

GLOSSARY

ABILITY TESTS. Tests of intelligence. These may consist of either verbal or non-verbal items, or both. Ability tests should not be confused with attainment tests. The latter are designed to measure the standard of skill reached in a subject. Each test is standardized on the whole population of children who took it after allowing for the original selection. The population mean is then 50 and standard deviation 10.

AGGREGATE TEST SCORES. The combined test score for a test battery. Aggregate test scores are available for each of the three ages, eight, eleven and fifteen. It is a measure of both intelligence and attainment. Each aggregate test score was obtained by adding the four standardized scores of a test battery together and then restandardizing these summed scores on the population of pupils that had sat all three sets of tests, after allowing for the original selection. The mean of these standardized scores is 50 and the standard deviation 9·5.

ATTAINMENT TESTS. Tests measuring the standard of work a pupil has attained. At fifteen years, the attainment tests were mathematics and reading. Each test is standardized on the whole population of children who take it after allowing for the original selection. The population mean is then 50 and the standard deviation 10.

BORDERLINE PUPILS. Those pupils having aggregate test scores of 55–59 at fifteen years. The term was originally used to describe those pupils who were at the borderline level of entry to grammar school.

EDUCATIONAL SAMPLE. Those pupils tested at all three ages, eight, eleven and fifteen years.

GOOD 'O' LEVEL CERTIFICATE. A certificate which has at least four passes, covering at least three of the main academic fields: English language, mathematics, a science subject and a foreign language, excluding Welsh.

HIGH ABILITY PUPILS. Pupils of high ability—those having aggregate test scores of 60 or more in the fifteen year tests, i.e. in the top 16% in test performance.

MAUDSLEY PERSONALITY INVENTORY (MPI). This was the short scale of 6 questions designed to give a rough-and-ready measure of neuroticism (or emotionality). See Eysenck, 1958.

NON-VERBAL TEST. A test of intelligence which consists of pictures or diagrams as opposed to words.

[192]

OVER-ACHIEVING. A general term used when the results of the attainment tests (reading and mathematics) are above those of non-verbal intelligence.

PICTURE INTELLIGENCE. The non-verbal test of intelligence used at eight years.

POPULATION ESTIMATES. These are population rates calculated by restoring the original balance of the follow-up sample, i.e. allowance is made for the fact that only one in four of the manual working class families was included.

SESSION 1961/2 (COMPLETED). Those staying on at school or technical college at least to finish the academic year after their sixteenth birthdays. Many pupils would have taken their G.C.E. 'O' level examination that summer after a five-year course (four years in Scotland).

SESSION 1962/3 (STARTED). Those who stayed at school or technical college at least to start the September term 1962. For many (but not in Scotland), this would be the start of a sixth form course.

STANDARD DEVIATION. A technical term which measures the scatter or dispersion of scores or results. In this study, the standard deviation of the individual tests was 10, i.e. 68 per cent of the population have scores between 41 and 59, leaving 16 per cent with scores above and 16 per cent below these limits.

UNDER-ACHIEVING. A general term used when the results of the attainment tests (reading and mathematics) are below those of the non-verbal intelligence.

VERBAL TEST. An intelligence test measuring the understanding and use of words.

Appendix I

Details of the Fifteen Year Tests

Douglas Pidgeon

National Foundation for Educational Research in
England and Wales

As in the earlier surveys, severe restrictions were imposed upon the
choice of tests; they had necessarily to be short—it was undesirable
to remove the Survey pupils for too long a period from their school
work; they also needed to be easy to administer since, for the most
part, they would be given by teachers in groups varying in size
from 1 to 12 or more; they also need to be 'wide-range' to cover
the variations in performance expected from a representative
sample of fifteen-year-olds. In order to maintain continuity from
the earlier surveys it was decided that the test battery should included
both a verbal and a non-verbal ability test as well as tests of reading
and mathematics.

The tests finally decided upon were:

*Group Ability Test AH*4 by A. W. Heim, M.A., Ph.D.

This test has separate verbal and non-verbal sections, each
consisting of 65 items of various types. Each section is preceded by
a short practice test and has a working time limit of 10 minutes.
Total time for administration is about 30 minutes.

The Watts-Vernon Reading Test

This 35 item test of reading comprehension has been used ex-
tensively in the Ministry of Education surveys of reading. Working
time is 10 minutes, with total administration time of about 15
minutes.

[194]

Mathematics Test

This test was especially constructed for the Survey. It contained 47 items similar in kind to the Graded Arithmetic-Mathematics Test by P. E. Vernon. It was however structured as a continuous test. Most of the items could be solved mentally if the principle was understood. The working time, established after trials during construction, was 25 minutes, with total administration time of about 30 minutes.

To ease administration the three tests were combined into a single booklet which also included at the beginning a two-page questionnaire and at the end the Rothwell-Miller Interest Blank. The tests were timed separately and, in order to arrange the pages appropriately so that the testees would not be faced with the last page of one test and the first page of the next open together, it was necessary to reverse the usual order of presenting the two parts of the Heim test. There was no evidence however that taking the non-verbal part first before the verbal part in any way influenced performance.

A separate booklet giving detailed instructions for the administration of the tests was provided for the teachers and the recommendation was made that the testing should be carried out in two separate sessions—on the mornings of two consecutive days; the questionnaire and the general ability test on the first occasion and the reading and mathematics tests and Interest Blank on the second. This procedure appeared to be followed by nearly all of the schools concerned. The test booklets were returned to the National Foundation where the tests were marked and check marked. Weighted norms were calculated from the data obtained, for converting the raw scores to T-scores with a mean of 50 and a standard deviation of 10.

Reliability of the Tests

Reliabilities were calculated using Kuder-Richardson Formula 20 from a sub-sample of 252 booklets drawn at random from all those used in the Survey. The distribution of raw scores on each test obtained from this sub-sample was compared with the distributions of total *weighted* raw scores derived from the whole sample and was found to be very similar. In view of this, the figures given below can be considered to be reasonable estimates.

Test	Reliability (K–R 20)
AH4 Non-Verbal	0·93
AH4 Verbal	0·94
AH4 Total	0·96
Reading	0·91
Mathematics	0·89

Further information on the reliability of the Heim and the Watts-Vernon tests is given in published literature. The manual to the AH4 test* quotes a figure of 0·92 for a test-retest consistency of total score with an interval of one month. For the reading test, the Ministry of Education† give a figure of 0·89 for its reliability (K–R Formula 20) derived from a sample of fifteen year olds, and Morris‡ quotes a similar figure for a test-retest coefficient obtained from her sample of eleven year olds.

Validity of the Tests

Independent evidence on the validity of the general ability test for its intended purpose in this survey is difficult to obtain. The manual (op. cit.) quotes correlations around 0·6 and 0·7 with other similar tests and gives evidence of association between scores on AH4 and criteria such as examination performance. Perhaps the best evidence of the test's validity in this Survey however comes from the results produced. There are many instances described in the main text where scores on AH4—both verbal and non-verbal as well as total—conform precisely to what would be expected if the test was indeed giving a valid measure of the abilities it purports to assess. Confirmation of the expected increases the confidence with which the unexpected can be received.

The validity of the achievement tests is best stated in terms of their content and this can be demonstrated by reproducing them. Unfortunately they are research instruments and to publish them would endanger their usefulness for future surveys. The validity of

* *AH4 Group Test of General Intelligence, Manual.* A. W. Heim, N.F.E.R. Revised Edition (1967).

† *Reading Ability: Some Suggestions for Helping the Backward.* Ministry of Education Pamphlet No. 18. London: H.M. Stationery Office (1950).

‡ *Standards and Progress in Reading.* Joyce M. Morris, N.F.E.R. (1966).

the reading test has been fully discussed elsewhere* and it may merely be noted that it has amply proved its effectiveness in the kind of survey for which it has been used on this occasion. It is of interest to note that the correlations of the fifteen-year-old reading test scores with the scores obtained on the reading and vocabulary tests given at age eight varied between 0·63 and 0·69, and with the similar tests given at age eleven from 0·72 to 0·76. The mathematics test was new and therefore no independent evidence on its validity exists, apart from the correlations of 0·82 and 0·80 for boys and girls respectively with the arithmetic test given to the same survey children at the age of eleven. The other inter-correlations of the tests used in this Survey and those used in the surveys at ages eight and eleven are given in the additional volume of tables deposited in the Copyright Libraries (see page 201).

Reference may finally be made to the actual performance of the tests in the Survey. The table below gives the mean weighted scores for each test together with its standard deviation.

Test	No. items	Weighted mean score	Standard deviation
AH4 Non-Verbal	65	37·77	10·58
AH4 Verbal	65	33·92	11·51
AH4 Total	130	71·57	20·07
Reading	35	23·53	6·75
Mathematics	47	12·62	9·61

It can be seen that the reading test was somewhat on the easy side, although the mean score compares favourably with the national population estimates derived from the 1961 D.E.S. survey (op. cit.). On the assumption of a consistent gain in reading score for pupils in all types of school between 1956 and 1961, it was estimated that the national population mean score for all fifteen year olds in 1961 was approximately 24·1. The mean score of the survey pupils was in fact 23·5.

The mathematics test was clearly too difficult, the distribution of raw scores being severely positively skewed. While this was unfortunate and makes this test the least satisfactory of those used, it has probably not had a serious effect upon the results obtained.

* *Progress in Reading*. Department of Education and Science, Education Pamphlet No. 50. H.M. Stationery Office (1966).

Appendix II

Ages at which Information was Collected

Interview with mother—eight weeks, two, four, six, seven, eight, nine, eleven, fifteen years.

Medical examination—six, seven, eleven, fifteen years.

School teacher reports—seven, ten, thirteen, fifteen, sixteen years.

Tests—eight, eleven, fifteen years.

Questionnaire completed by Survey member—thirteen, fifteen years.

Running absence records—six and a half to ten and a half years.

Head teachers' forms—eleven, fifteen years.

Appendix III

Social Class Classification in the National Survey

The classification is based, for the most part, on the 1957 occupation of the father of the Survey child; where this is not known, on the 1946 occupation.

Upper Middle Class
The father is a non-manual worker, and
(a) both parents went to secondary school and were brought up in middle class families, or
(b) both parents went to secondary school and one parent was brought up in a middle class family, or
(c) both parents were brought up in middle class families and one parent went to secondary school.

Lower Middle Class
The rest of the non-manual workers' families.

Upper Manual Working Class
The father is a manual worker and
either the father or mother or both of them had a secondary school education, and/or one or both of them were brought up in a middle class family.

Lower Manual Working Class
The father is a manual worker, and
both the father and the mother had elementary schooling only, and both the father and the mother were brought up in manual working class families.

[199]

Appendix IV

Boys: Assessment of Maturity

These assessments are based on the following questions in the school doctors' examination forms completed when the boys were fifteen.

Is any pigmented pubic hair visible?   Yes, sparse
                                             Yes, profuse
                                             No

Is any axillary hair visible?   Yes
                                             No

Has the child's voice broken?   Not yet broken
                                             Starting to break
                                             Completely broken

Development of genitalia   Infantile
                                             Early*
                                             Advanced or complete†

The four maturity groups are as follows:

Mature—fully broken voice, axillary hair, profuse pubic hair, mature genitals (24·5 per cent of sample).

Advanced signs—genitals assessed as mature but one of the other maturity signs absent (30·0 per cent of sample).

Early signs—intermediate between advanced and infantile (35·1 per cent of sample).

Infantile—infantile genitals, no pubic or axillary hair, voice unbroken (10·4 per cent of sample).

* Early: Increase in length of penis and width of glans with softening and slight enlargement of testes.

† Advanced: Substantial enlargment of glans and penis plus testicular enlargement with pendulous and rugose scrotum.

Appendix V

The following libraries hold a companion volume of full and detailed tables which form the basis of the statements made in this book:

The University Library, University of Cambridge.

The Library, Trinity College, University of Dublin.

The National Library of Scotland, Edinburgh 1.

The British Museum, Department of Printed Books, London, W.C.1.

The Library, London School of Economics, London, W.C.2.

The Library, University of Manchester, Manchester 13.

The Bodleian Library, Department of Printed Books, Oxford.

The National Library of Wales, Aberystwyth, Cardiganshire.

Some of the more important tables from this volume are given in this appendix.

TABLE 1

LOSSES FROM THE SURVEY

	Actual numbers	% of those living in this country
Living in England, Wales and Scotland in 1962		
(a) Full test information	3,626	76·8
(b) Test information in 1 or 2 years	757	16·0
(c) No test information*	337	7·1
TOTAL	4,720	
Dead or Abroad	642	
TOTAL	5,362	

* Includes those in E.S.N. schools and institutions who took none of the tests.

[201]

TABLE 2

SOCIAL CLASS, LEAVING DATE, G.C.E. 'O' LEVEL RESULTS AND TYPE OF SCHOOL

Based on population estimates except for social class

PERCENTAGE DISTRIBUTIONS

	Boys		Girls	
	Educational Sample*	Complete Sample†	Educational Sample*	Complete Sample†
(a) *Social Class*				
Middle { Upper	11	11	10	11
Middle { Lower	31	32	30	31
Manual { Upper	17	17	18	18
Manual { Lower	41	40	42	41
TOTAL %	100	100	100	101
(b) *Leaving School*				
At 15 years	48	47	51	51
Between 15 and 16¼ years	27	27	26	24
After 16¼ years	25	26	23	25
TOTAL %	100	100	100	100
(c) *'O' Level Certificates*				
Good certificates	13	12	10	9
Other certificates	13	13	14	14
No certificates	74	75	76	77
TOTAL %	100	100	100	100
(d) *Type of School*				
Grammar	19	18	20	19
Direct Grant	2	2	2	2
Technical	4	4	3	3
Secondary Modern	61	59	59	57
Comprehensive	10	10	12	12
Independent	2	4	4	6
Ineducable, Special and Approved	2	3	1	2
TOTAL %	100	100	101	101

* The Educational Sample—those who completed all three sets of educational tests at eight, eleven and fifteen years.

† The Complete Sample—the Educational Sample plus all those with available information.

[202]

TABLE 3

MEAN AGGREGATE TEST SCORES

Population estimates

MEAN SCORES

| | Boys | | Girls | |
Age of Testing	Educational Sample*	Complete Sample†	Educational Sample*	Complete Sample†
8	49·7	49·4	50·1	49·9
11	49·8	49·6	50·2	50·2
15	50·6	50·5	49·3	49·1

* The Educational Sample—those who completed all three sets of educational tests at eight, eleven and fifteen years.
† The Complete Sample—the Educational Sample plus all those with available information.

[203]

TABLE 4

PROPORTIONS STAYING AT SCHOOL AND GAINING
CERTIFICATES RELATED TO ABILITY AND SOCIAL CLASS

PERCENTAGE TABLE

		Ability at 15 years				
Social Class		60 and over	55–59	50–54	45–49	44 and less
		% completing session 1961–2				
Middle	Upper	97	93	86	69	40
	Lower	94	79	59	36	17
Manual	Upper	90	67	35	22	6
	Lower	80	46	27	12	3
		% starting session 1962–3				
Middle	Upper	90	82	71	42	20
	Lower	78	52	37	20	8
Manual	Upper	67	43	20	10	3
	Lower	50	20	12	4	2
		% gaining good certificates				
Middle	Upper	77	33	11	4	—
	Lower	60	18	6	—	—
Manual	Upper	53	15	2	1	—
	Lower	37	9	3	—	—
		% gaining general certificates				
Middle	Upper	94	79	54	27	20
	Lower	87	59	38	13	1
Manual	Upper	86	45	17	5	—
	Lower	69	31	12	2	—

[204]

TABLE 5

TEST SCORES OF BOYS AND GIRLS

Population estimates

MEAN SCORES

	Picture intelligence	Vocabulary	Reading	Sentence completion	Aggregate
8 years					
Boys	50·2	50·7	49·7	49·8	49·7
Girls	50·3	49·8	50·9	50·9	50·1

	Intelligence Non-verbal	Verbal	Vocabulary	Reading	Arithmetic	Aggregate
11 years						
Boys	49·9	49·0	50·6	49·9	50·0	49·8
Girls	50·2	51·3	49·5	50·4	50·5	50·2

	Intelligence Non-verbal	Verbal	Reading	Mathematics	Aggregate
15 years					
Boys	51·5	49·7	51·0	51·6	50·6
Girls	49·8	50·7	50·3	48·6	49·3

TABLE 6

PROPORTIONS GAINING GENERAL CERTIFICATES AT EACH LEVEL OF ABILITY

PERCENTAGE TABLE

	Boys		Girls	
Ability at 15 years	Good certificates	All certificates	Good certificates	All certificates
00–44	—	—	—	1
45–49	1*	4	—	9
50–54	4	21	4	28
55–59	18	48	16	53
60 and over	58	86	62	85

* E.g. of boys with aggregate test scores of 45–49, 1 per cent gained good certificates.

[205]

TABLE 7

ADJUSTED* TEST SCORES OF PUPILS AT SELECTIVE SCHOOLS

MEAN SCORES

Graduate staff	Intelligence, total		Arithmetic and mathematics		Reading	
	11	15	11	15	11	15
<70%	56·4	55·8	55·8	56·7	56·1	56·6
70–79%	59·7	58·1	61·1	60·2	59·2	59·5
80% or more	60·6	59·2	61·1	61·0	60·5	60·7

* Adjusted for sex and social class.

TABLE 8

ADJUSTED† TEST SCORES OF PUPILS AT SELECTIVE SCHOOLS RELATED TO SOCIAL CLASS

MEAN SCORES

Social class		Intelligence, total		Arithmetic and mathematics		Reading	
		11	15	11	15	11	15
Middle	Upper	59·6	58·6	58·9	61·0	60·0	60·6
	Lower	59·3	57·8	59·5	59·6	59·0	59·2
Manual	Upper	59·1	57·4	59·7	58·5	57·8	58·4
	Lower	57·8	57·4	59·7	57·9	57·4	57·8

† Adjusted for sex and type of school.

TABLE 9

THE DIFFERENCES BETWEEN THE ADJUSTED‡ FIFTEEN-YEAR INTELLIGENCE AND ATTAINMENT TEST SCORES FOR THOSE AT SELECTIVE SCHOOLS

MEAN DIFFERENCES

Social class		Mathematics minus intelligence	Reading minus intelligence
Middle	Upper	+2·4	+2·0
	Lower	+1·8	+1·4
Manual	Upper	+1·1	+1·1
	Lower	+0·5	+0·4

‡ Adjusted for sex and type of school.

[206]

TABLE 10

GENERAL CERTIFICATES AND LEAVING AGE RELATED TO
SOCIAL CLASS AND TYPE OF SELECTIVE SCHOOL

PERCENTAGE TABLE

Graduate staff		Middle Upper (a)	Lower (b)	Manual Upper (c)	Lower (d)	Ratio (a):(d)
		% gaining good certificates				
<70%	Actual	37	30	21	11	3·3
	Expected*	31	26	22	24	1·3
70–79%	Actual	61	38	32	31	2·0
	Expected*	47	39	41	39	1·2
80% or more	Actual	60	50	48	39	1·5
	Expected*	51	51	52	45	1·1
		% gaining general certificates				
<70%	Actual	76	65	48	37	2·1
	Expected*	63	65	56	56	1·1
70–79%	Actual	91	81	81	75	1·2
	Expected*	85	81	82	82	1·0
80% or more	Actual	89	85	81	78	1·1
	Expected*	84	84	84	81	1·0
		% starting session 1962/3				
<70%	Actual	85	65	48	28	3·0
	Expected*	61	59	57	58	1·0
70–79%	Actual	92	71	62	56	1·6
	Expected*	74	73	71	71	1·0
80% or more	Actual	93	76	67	54	1·7
	Expected*	76	76	76	73	1·0

* The expected rates were calculated on the assumption that at each level of
ability and for each sex the chances of getting a certificate or of being at school
at sixteen and a half years were (for each type of school considered separately)
unrelated to social class.

[207]

TABLE 11

ADJUSTED* TEST SCORES OF PUPILS AT SECONDARY
MODERN SCHOOLS

MEAN SCORES

Past record of school	Intelligence, total		Arithmetic and mathematics		Reading	
	11	15	11	15	11	15
Poor	46·5	47·3	46·6	46·2	46·8	46·8
Fair	46·5	47·1	46·1	46·4	46·5	47·3
Good	47·9	47·6	46·9	47·2	47·2	48·4

* Adjusted for sex and social class.

TABLE 12

DIFFERENCES BETWEEN THE ADJUSTED† FIFTEEN-YEAR
INTELLIGENCE AND ATTAINMENT TEST SCORES FOR THOSE
AT SECONDARY MODERN SCHOOLS

MEAN DIFFERENCES

Past record of school	Mathematics minus intelligence	Reading minus intelligence
Poor	−1·0	−0·5
Fair	−0·8	+0·1
Good	−0·4	+0·8

† Adjusted for sex and social class.

[208]

TABLE 13

ADJUSTED* TEST SCORES OF PUPILS AT SECONDARY
MODERN SCHOOLS RELATED TO SOCIAL CLASS

MEAN SCORES

Social Class		Intelligence, total		Arithmetic and mathematics		Reading	
		11	15	11	15	11	15
Middle		49·4	49·6	48·6	48·6	49·2	50·2
Manual {	Upper	47·2	47·2	47·3	47·2	47·4	48·0
	Lower	46·0	46·5	45·5	45·7	45·7	46·3

*Adjusted for sex and type of school.

[209]

TABLE 14

GENERAL CERTIFICATES AND LEAVING AGE RELATED
TO SOCIAL CLASS AND TYPE OF SECONDARY MODERN
SCHOOL

PERCENTAGE TABLE

Past record of school		Middle (a)	Upper manual (b)	Lower manual (c)	Ratio (a): (c)
		% gaining certificates			
Poor	Actual	6	1	†	28·0
	Expected*	2	1	1	1·9
Fair	Actual	7	6	3	2·1
	Expected*	8	5	4	2·0
Good	Actual	19	5	7	2·9
	Expected*	12	9	9	1·5
		% completing the session 1961/2			
Poor	Actual	20	9	5	3·9
	Expected*	11	8	7	1·5
Fair	Actual	29	20	9	3·2
	Expected*	20	17	14	1·4
Good	Actual	40	22	19	2·1
	Expected*	30	25	24	1·2
		% staying after statutory leaving age			
Poor	Actual	40	15	15	2·7
	Expected*	27	14	18	1·5
Fair	Actual	53	36	21	2·5
	Expected*	37	32	28	1·3
Good	Actual	62	44	37	1·7
	Expected*	51	46	44	1·2

* The expected rates were calculated on the assumption that at each level of ability and for each sex the chances of getting a certificate or of staying at school were (for each type of school considered separately) the same in each social class.

† <0·5 per cent.

TABLE 15

GENERAL CERTIFICATES AND LEAVING AGE OF PUPILS RELATED TO TYPE OF INDEPENDENT SCHOOL

PERCENTAGE TABLE

(a) *Boys in schools that were members or*
non-members of the Headmasters' Conference

	Member			Non-Member		
Ability at 15 years	Good certificates	All certificates	Started session 1962/3	Good certificates	All certificates	Started session 1962/3
00–54	11*	67	89	—	22	44
55–59	33	67	92	6	50	63
60 and over	83	94	94	59	68	73
All	55	80	92	19	40	61

(b) *Girls in schools that were members or*
non-members of the Association of Headmistresses

	Member			Non-Member		
00–54	7	54	79	2	29	43
55–59	47	80	93	3	32	52
60 and over	42	67	83	28	56	53
All	35	71	85	7	34	50

* E.g. of boys at Headmasters' Conference schools with aggregate test scores of 54 and below 11 per cent gained good certificates.

TABLE 16

GENERAL CERTIFICATES AND LEAVING AGE OF (A) BOYS
IN HEADMASTERS' CONFERENCE INDEPENDENT SCHOOLS
AND (B) UPPER MIDDLE CLASS BOYS IN GRAMMAR SCHOOLS

PERCENTAGE TABLE

Ability at 15 years	Headmasters' Conference independent			Upper middle-class grammar		
	Good certificates	All certificates	Started session 1962/3	Good certificates	All certificates	Started session 1962/3
00–54	11*	67	89	25	62	100
55–59	33	67	92	44	81	78
60 and over	83	94	94	82	95	95
All	55	80	92	66	88	90

* E.g. of boys at Headmasters' Conference schools with aggregate test scores of 54 and below 11 per cent gained good certificates.

TABLE 17

PROPORTION OF PUPILS AT SINGLE SEX AND MIXED
GRAMMAR SCHOOLS STARTING THE SESSION 1962/3

PERCENTAGE TABLE

Type of school and age of puberty	Boys	Girls
	% starting session 1962/3	
Single sex schools { Later puberty	74	81
Earlier puberty	78	68
Mixed sex schools { Later puberty	68	71
Earlier puberty	73	76

TABLE 18

GOOD CERTIFICATES, LEAVING AGE AND WISHES FOR
HIGHER EDUCATION IN SCOTLAND AND ENGLAND AND
WALES

PERCENTAGE TABLE

Achievement and progress	Scotland	England and Wales
Stayed after statutory leaving age	55*	59
Started session 1962/3	31	31
All certificates	30	33
Good certificates	16	16
Wants further education	27	24

* E.g. of pupils living in Scotland 55 per cent stayed after the statutory
leaving age.

TABLE 19

GENERAL CERTIFICATES AND LEAVING AGE RELATED TO
AVAILABILITY OF SELECTIVE SCHOOL PLACES IN ENGLAND
AND WALES

Population estimates

PERCENTAGE TABLE

	Selective school places available for:		
	13–23%	24 or 25%	26–36%
(a) Boys			
Stayed after statutory leaving age	48†	49	61
Completed session 1961/2	38	36	43
Started session 1962/3	21	24	29
General certificates { Good	12	12	13
All	25	24	27
(b) Girls			
Stayed after statutory leaving age	40	51	43
Completed session 1961/2	32	36	44
Started session 1962/3	18	23	31
General certificates { Good	10	10	11
All	21	25	27

† E.g. of pupils living in areas providing 13–23 per cent of selective school
places for their pupils, 48 per cent stayed after the statutory leaving age.

TABLE 20

PARENTAL INTEREST AND WISHES FOR HIGHER EDUCATION
RELATED TO EDUCATION OF BOTH PARENTS

PERCENTAGE TABLE

Education of both parents

	Both elementary	Elementary, plus some further effort	One or both secondary	Both secondary, plus some further effort
	% with highly interested parents			
All pupils				
Middle	41	60	72	84
Manual	21	40	37	69
	% with mother favourable to higher education			
Ability 60 and over				
Middle	69	81	87	93
Manual	53	71	78	100

TABLE 21

PROPORTIONS OF PARENTS CHOOSING PROFESSIONAL JOBS
FOR THEIR CHILDREN RELATED TO SOCIAL CLASS AND
ABILITY

PERCENTAGE TABLE

	Middle		Manual	
	Upper	*Lower*	*Upper*	*Lower*
	% with parents choosing professional jobs for their children			
Ability 60 and over				
Boys	79	61	47	39
Girls	71	55	57	35
	% with parents choosing professional jobs for their children			
Ability 50–59				
Boys	48	28	17	7
Girls	47	28	29	14

[214]

TABLE 22

GENERAL CERTIFICATES AND LEAVING AGE RELATED TO PARENTS' HEALTH

PERCENTAGE TABLE

	Both good	Parents' health Intermediate	One or both poor
		% gaining good certificates	
Ability 60 and over			
Middle	70	67	60
Manual	49	41	44
		% gaining certificates at any level	
Middle	88	92	87
Manual	82	80	70
		% gaining good certificates	
Ability 50–59			
Middle	17	17	13
Manual	6	5	7
		% gaining certificates at any level	
Middle	54	57	53
Manual	27	23	24
		% starting the session 1962/3	
Selective school pupils			
Middle	84	76	77
Manual	63	51	48
		% completing the session 1961/2	
Secondary modern school pupils			
Middle	36	35	26
Manual	18	13	8

[215]

TABLE 23

TEST SCORES RELATED TO FATHERS' UNEMPLOYMENT THROUGH ILLNESS

Population estimates

MEAN SCORES

	Unemployed through illness	All employed
(a) *Tests at*		
8	43·6	50·1
11	44·3	50·2
15	44·6	50·2
(b) *Test scores at 15*		
Non-verbal	46·5	50·8
Verbal	46·1	50·3
Mathematics	45·2	50·4
Reading	45·7	50·8

TABLE 24

TEST SCORES AT FIFTEEN RELATED TO DEATH OF FATHER

Population estimates

MEAN SCORES

	Sudden death		Death after long illness	
	Child under 6	Child 6 or older	Child under 6	Child 6 or older
Test scores				
Non-verbal	52·3	50·7	46·9	43·2
Verbal	51·0	51·2	46·2	45·4
Mathematics	51·2	49·6	46·3	44·0
Reading	50·7	49·8	47·3	46·9

MEAN DIFFERENCES

	Sudden death		Death after long illness	
Difference between observed and expected* aggregate test scores at 15	+2·4	−0·1	−1·7	−5·5
	+0·6		−3·0	

* I.e. expected after adjusting for social class, family size, standard of housing and standard of maternal care.

[216]

TABLE 25

PROPORTIONS OF (a) PUPILS HOPING TO ENTER THE
PROFESSIONS AND (b) BOYS HOPING TO ENTER
MANUAL WORK RELATED TO SOCIAL CLASS AND ABILITY

PERCENTAGE TABLE

	Middle		Manual	
	Upper	*Lower*	*Upper*	*Lower*
Ability at 15	*% hoping to enter the professions*			
(a) *Boys*				
60 and over	79	61	47	39
55–59	48	28	17	7
50–54	†	12	2	5
	% hoping to enter the professions			
Girls				
60 and over	71	55	57	35
55–59	47	28	29	14
50–54	†	15	9	7
	% hoping to enter manual work			
(b) *Boys*				
60 and over	7	15	18	26
55–59	5	33	44	56
50–54	†	36	54	65
45–49	†	52	57	68
0–44	†	62	65	82

† < 20 pupils.

[217]

TABLE 26

TEST SCORES RELATED TO A COMBINATION OF NEUROTICISM, BEHAVIOUR RATINGS AND SYMPTOMS AT FIFTEEN

Population estimates

MEAN SCORES

	Neuroticism scores					
	High Behaviour ratings and symptoms			Other Behaviour ratings and symptoms		
	High	*Average*	*Low*	*High*	*Average*	*Low*
Aggregate test scores at						
8	46·2	49·4	51·2	48·6	50·6	52·1
11	45·9	49·2	51·8	48·4	50·8	52·9
15	45·2	49·9	51·6	48·1	51·1	53·3
Test scores at 15						
Non-verbal	47·8	50·8	51·2	49·1	51·5	53·1
Verbal	45·7	50·3	51·9	48·4	51·1	52·6
Mathematics	46·3	49·7	52·2	48·3	50·9	53·7
Reading	45·6	50·6	51·7	49·3	51·8	53·3
Percentage of sample (percentaged across)	6	14	13	18	33	16

[218]

TABLE 27

GENERAL CERTIFICATES AND LEAVING AGE RELATED TO A COMBINATION OF NEUROTICISM, BEHAVIOUR RATINGS AND SYMPTOMS AT FIFTEEN

PERCENTAGE TABLE

	Neuroticism scores					
	High Behaviour ratings and symptoms			*Other* Behaviour ratings and symptoms		
	High	*Average*	*Low*	*High*	*Average*	*Low*
Ability 60 and over						
General ⎰ Good	47*	52	41	42	62	65
Certificates ⎱ All	79	86	78	81	85	88
Ability 50–59						
General ⎰ Good	5	6	8	8	10	17
Certificates ⎱ All	28	29	33	36	39	38
Selective school pupils Started session 1962/3	61	78	70	66	73	75
Secondary modern school pupils Completed session 1961/2	9	14	26	13	22	26

* E.g. of pupils with high neuroticism and behaviour scores 47 per cent of those of high ability gained good certificates.

[219]

TABLE 28

SOME CHARACTERISTICS OF THE FAMILIES OF
DELINQUENT BOYS

PERCENTAGE TABLE

Type of offence

	Trivial	Serious	Repeaters	Expected†
Low parental interest	54*	65	70	45
No post-natal services used	15	23	32	17
Poor maternal care	41	59	78	41
Separated from mother for one week or more in first 4½ years	26	36	41	32
Shared bed (11 years)	59	67	79	59
Overcrowded (15 years)	38	47	73	37
Lacking home amenities (15 years)	22	33	29	26
In council house (15 years)	44	41	62	46
Large family (4 or more)	42	44	71	36
Broken family (divorce or separation)	6	15	11	5
Broken family (death)	7	6	4	7
Father frequently away	12	9	16	9
Mother employed (11 years)	58	57	62	60

* E.g. of trivial offenders 54 per cent had parents who took little interest in their school work.

† These percentages were obtained by applying the social class composition of the delinquents to the whole sample of boys.

TABLE 29

TEST SCORES OF DELINQUENT AND NON-DELINQUENT BOYS

Population estimates

MEAN SCORES

	Type of offence			Non-
	Trivial	Serious	Repeaters	Delinquents
Aggregate test scores at				
8	46·0	46·8	42·9	50·3
11	47·0	46·4	41·5	50·5
15	46·7	46·6	42·7	51·4
Differences between observed and expected* score at 15	−2·7	−2·2	−4·2	—
Test scores at 15				
Non-verbal	48·4	50·0	46·6	51·9
Verbal	45·7	47·1	43·2	50·3
Mathematics	47·9	46·5	45·0	51·7
Reading	48·0	46·1	42·9	52·3

* I.e. expected after adjusting for social class, family size, standard of housing and standard of maternal care.

TABLE 30

AGGREGATE TEST SCORES RELATED TO FAMILY SIZE

Population estimates

MEAN SCORES

	One	Family size Two	Three	Four or more
Test scores at				
Middle				
8	56·3	56·0	54·5	52·5
11	56·5	56·6	54·9	53·2
15	56·4	56·2	54·8	52·4
Manual				
8	51·7	50·4	48·7	45·6
11	51·5	50·2	48·6	45·7
15	51·2	49·7	49·0	46·2

[221]

TABLE 31

TEST SCORES AT EIGHT AND FIFTEEN RELATED TO NUMBER OF OTHER PRE-SCHOOL CHILDREN IN THE FAMILY, 1946–50—PUPILS IN THREE-CHILD MIDDLE CLASS FAMILIES

Population estimates

MEAN SCORES

Age and type of test	Number of pre-school children in family (other than survey child), 1946–50		
	None	One	Two
8 years			
Picture intelligence	53·6	54·8	53·8
Vocabulary	57·2	53·6	51·9
15 years			
Non-verbal intelligence	53·8	54·2	54·8
Reading	56·2	55·0	52·7

TABLE 32

PROPORTIONS STAYING AFTER STATUTORY LEAVING AGE RELATED TO FAMILY SIZE AND ABILITY

PERCENTAGE TABLE

		Family size		Four or
	One	Two	Three	more
	% staying after statutory leaving age			
Ability at 15				
60 and over	99	97	94	92
55–59	89	85	82	72
50–54	73	71	71	49
45–49	54	50	41	24
0–44	22	24	24	20

TABLE 33

TEST SCORES OF BOYS IN TWO-CHILD FAMILIES

Population estimates

	MEAN SCORES	
	Elder	Younger
Non-verbal tests at		
8	52·2	52·1
11	51·0	51·5
15	52·3	52·0
Reading tests at		
8	53·4	50·5
11	54·5	51·0
15	55·2	52·1

TABLE 34

GENERAL CERTIFICATES, LEAVING AGE AND WISHES FOR HIGHER EDUCATION OF BOYS IN ONE- AND TWO-CHILD FAMILIES

PERCENTAGE TABLE

	Only	Elder	Younger
All Boys			
General ⎰ Good	20*	30	21
Certificates ⎱ All	39	48	42
Stayed after statutory leaving age	73	78	65
Started session 1962/3	40	45	39
Ability 60 and over—wishes for higher education			
Pupil—favourable	61	80	59
Teacher—favourable	89	85	86
Mother—favourable	90	88	83

* E.g. of boys who are only children 20 per cent gained good certificates.

[223]

TABLE 35

TEST SCORES OF BOYS IN TWO-CHILD FAMILIES RELATED
TO BIRTH INTERVAL

Population estimates

MEAN SCORES

	Birth interval		
	Not more than 2 years	2–4 years	More than 4 years
Non-verbal tests at			
8	52·6	53·0	51·4
11	50·6	52·1	50·9
15	52·5	52·3	51·8
Reading tests at			
8	52·2	52·9	50·6
11	51·9	53·9	51·7
15	53·2	54·4	52·8

TABLE 36

GENERAL CERTIFICATES AND LEAVING AGE OF THOSE
IN TWO-CHILD FAMILIES RELATED TO BIRTH INTERVAL

PERCENTAGE TABLE

	Birth interval		
	Not more than 2 years	2–4 years	More than 4 years
Boys			
General ⎰ Good	27*	30	21
Certificates ⎱ All	44	52	39
Stayed after statutory leaving age	69	77	66
Started session 1962/3	41	51	36
Girls			
General ⎰ Good	19	22	14
Certificates ⎱ All	38	44	37
Stayed after statutory leaving age	69	71	62
Started session 1962/3	35	46	34

* E.g. of boys with short birth intervals 27 per cent gained good certificates.

TABLE 37

GENERAL CERTIFICATES AND LEAVING AGE RELATED TO STAGE OF PUBERTY

PERCENTAGE TABLE

	Boys				Girls			
	Maturity at 15				Menarche			
	Mature	Advanced	Early signs	Infantile	—11 years 10 months	—12 years 10 months	—13 years 10 months	Later
Ability 60 and over								
General Certificates { Good	65*	50	59	52	78	66	59	51
General Certificates { All	91	85	84	79	100	87	84	78
Ability 50–59								
General Certificates { Good	16	10	8	11	12	7	12	13
General Certificates { All	35	36	30	35	36	40	40	47
Selective school pupils Started session 1962/3	74	72	73	65	59	71	68	72
Secondary modern school pupils Completed session 1961/2	19	19	16	12	26	23	17	14
Manual working-class pupils								
Selective school pupils Started session 1962/3	54	55	50	60	34	58	53	63
Secondary modern school pupils Completed session 1961/2	14	13	12	4	19	18	12	10

* E.g. of boys of high ability who were fully mature at fifteen, 65 per cent gained good certificates.

[225]

TABLE 38

PARENTS' EDUCATION AND PARENTAL INTEREST RELATED TO SHORT SIGHT

PERCENTAGE TABLE

	Normal vision	Short sight at 15
At secondary school		
Mother	18*	26
Father	22	35
At elementary school only but attempted		
further education		
Mother	19	30
Father	23	32
High parental interest		
Primary	36	44
Secondary	37	57
Father visited school	39	51
Separate room for homework	49	67
Good maternal care	29	33

* E.g. of pupils with normal vision 18 per cent had mothers who had been to secondary school.

TABLE 39

TEST SCORES* RELATED TO SHORT SIGHT

MEAN SCORES

	Normal vision	Short sight at 15 actual score	Standardized† scores
(a) *Aggregate test scores*			
Boys			
8	50·8	55·4	54·1
11	50·9	56·2	54·4
15	51·7	57·6	56·0
Girls			
8	51·1	55·5	55·1
11	51·1	57·0	56·6
15	50·3	55·9	55·5
(b) *Test scores at 15*			
Boys			
Non-verbal	52·0	55·7	54·9
Verbal	50·6	54·4	52·9
Mathematics	52·6	58·7	56·9
Reading	52·0	58·0	56·8
Girls			
Non-verbal	50·6	52·7	51·4
Verbal	51·5	56·4	56·2
Mathematics	49·7	54·8	54·4
Reading	50·9	57·0	56·6

* To avoid confusion with published figures (see Douglas, Ross and Simpson, 1967) these averages are based on actual numbers and not on population estimates.

† Standardized by social class.

TABLE 40

DIFFERENCES BETWEEN ACTUAL AND EXPECTED‡ READING SCORES RELATED TO THE ONSET OF SHORT SIGHT

MEAN DIFFERENCES

	Normal vision	Throughout	Short sight At 11 and 15	At 15 only
Test score differences at				
8	−0·4	+2·3	+2·7	+2·7
11	−0·2	+1·8	+2·0	+2·2
15	−0·3	+3·2	+4·5	+4·9

‡ The expected reading scores for each pupil at each age were calculated from regressing reading on non-verbal ability, the differences shown were obtained by deducting these expected scores from the observed reading scores.

TABLE 41

TEST SCORES AT FIFTEEN RELATED TO SECONDARY SCHOOL ABSENCE—SELECTIVE SCHOOL PUPILS, BOYS

Population estimates

MEAN SCORES

	Few	Absences Average	Many
Middle			
Non-verbal	55·8	55·9	56·2
Verbal	57·9	58·9	57·9
Mathematics	63·9	61·4	60·9
Reading	60·3	60·9	59·9
Manual			
Non-verbal	56·3	55·9	53·9
Verbal	58·9	58·6	56·3
Mathematics	62·0	59·2	56·9
Reading	59·4	57·8	56·6

TABLE 42

GENERAL CERTIFICATES AND LEAVING AGE RELATED TO SECONDARY SCHOOL ABSENCE AND TO SOCIAL CLASS—SECONDARY MODERN SCHOOL PUPILS

PERCENTAGE TABLE

	Boys Absences			Girls Absences		
	Few	Average	Many	Few	Average	Many
Middle						
Ability 50 and over						
General certificates—All	33*	25	23	20	25	15
Completed session 1961/2	40	26	27	54	24	22
Manual						
Ability 50 and over						
General certificates—All	11	4	6	16	8	6
Completed session 1961/2	19	9	6	25	14	7

* E.g. of middle class boys of average ability or above with few secondary school absences 33 per cent gained certificates.

[228]

TABLE 43

PROPORTIONS STAYING AT SCHOOL RELATED TO
SOME CHARACTERISTICS OF THE PARENTS AND
SCHOOLS—LOWER MANUAL WORKING-CLASS PUPILS
OF HIGH ABILITY

PERCENTAGE TABLE

		% starting the 1962/3 session	
		As specified	Others
Parents' characteristics			
Attempted further education { Mother		71*	44*
Father		67	46
Visited the school—Father		56	44
High parent interest		62	41
In good health { Mother		60	40
Father		56	43
Average or low neuroticism—Mother		54	39
Hoped child would enter professional work—Mother		80	25
Hoped child would enter higher education—Mother		71	22
Secondary modern schools characteristics			
Predominately middle class and skilled intake		22	11
20 per cent or more stayed after fifteen in past years		26	—
Good amenities		20	15
Good site		20	17
600 or more pupils		28	11
20 per cent more graduates		32	7
17 or less pupils per teacher		25	16

* E.g. of lower manual working-class pupils of high ability whose mothers
attempted further education 71% started the 1962/3 session compared with
44% of those whose mothers had not done so.

REFERENCES

BERNSTEIN, B. *A Socio-Linguistic Approach to Social Learning.* Penguin Survey of the Social Sciences, 1965. (Edited by J. Gould.) Penguin Books (1965).

BINET, A. and SIMON, T. *The Development of Intelligence in Children.* (Translated by E. S. Kitt.) Newlin, Baltimore (1916).

BURT, C. *Causes and Treatment of Backwardness.* University of London Press (1953).
   The Backward Child (4th edition). University of London Press (1958).

BUTLER, N. R. and BONHAM, D. G. *Perinatal Mortality.* E. & S. Livingstone (1963).

CENTRAL ADVISORY COUNCIL (FOR EDUCATION) (ENGLAND). *Children and their Primary Schools.* Her Majesty's Stationery Office (1967).
   Early Leaving. Her Majesty's Stationery Office (1954).
   15–18 (Volume I). Her Majesty's Stationery Office (1959).

COMMITTEE ON HIGHER EDUCATION. *Report.* Her Majesty's Stationery Office (1963).

DALE, R. R. 'A Critical Analysis of Research on the Effects of Co-Education on Academic Attainment in Grammar Schools—1.' *Educational Research* (1962), **4,** p. 207.
   'Co-Education: The Verdict of Experience, I.' *British Journal of Educational Psychology* (1955), **25,** p. 111.
   'Co-Education: The Verdict of Experience, II.' *British Journal of Educational Psychology* (1965), **35,** p. 195.

DANCY, J. *The Public Schools and the Future.* Faber & Faber (1963).

DEPARTMENT OF EDUCATION AND SCIENCE. *The Health of the School Child* (1962 and 1963). Her Majesty's Stationery Office (1964).

DEUTSCH, M. and BROWN, B. 'Social Influences in Negro-White Intelligence Differences.' *Journal of Sociological Issues* (1964), **20,** p. 24.

DOUGLAS, J. W. B. *The Home and the School.* MacGibbon & Kee (1964).

DOUGLAS, J. W. B. (1965). See Survey References, I. 10.

DOUGLAS, J. W. B. and ROSS, J. M. (1965). See Survey References I. 3.

DOUGLAS, J. W. B., ROSS, J. M., HAMMOND, W. H., and MULLIGAN, D. G. (1966). See Survey References II. 5.

EYSENCK, H. J. A short questionnaire for the Measurement of Two Dimensions of Personality. *J. Applied Psychology* (1958), **42,** p. 14.

HOLLY, D. N. 'Profiting from a Comprehensive School: Class, Sex and Ability.' *British Journal of Sociology* (1965), **16,** p. 150.

[230]

HOROBIN, G., OLDMAN, D., and BYTHEWAY, B. 'The Social Differentiation of Ability.' *Sociology* (1967), **1**, p. 113.

INGRAM, T. T. S. and REID, J. F. 'Developmental Aphasia Observed in a Department of Child Psychology.' *Archives of Disease in Childhood* (1956), **31**, p. 161.

JAHODA, G. 'Refractive Errors, Intelligence and Social Mobility.' *British Journal of Social and Clinical Psychology* (1962), **1**, p. 96.

JOINT COMMITTEE (of the Royal College of Obstetricians and Gynaecologists and the Population Investigation Committee). *Maternity in Great Britain.* Oxford University Press (1948).

KALTON, G. *The Public Schools.* Longmans (1966).

MARRO. (Quoted by Niceforo, A. Les Classes Pauvres. Paris, Giard & Briere (1905).) *La Puberta.* Turin (1900).

MASTERS, P. L. and HOCKEY, S. W. 'National Reserves of Ability—Some Evidence from Independent Schools.' *The Times Educational Supplement* (1963), 17th May, p. 1061.

MAXWELL, J. *The Level and Trend of National Intelligence.* University of London Press (1961).

MORRIS, J. N. and HEADY, J. A. 'Social and Biological Factors in Infant Mortality: V. Mortality in Relation to the Father's Occupation 1911–1950.' *Lancet* (1955), **i**, p. 554.

MULLIGAN, D. G. (1964). Survey References II, 6.

NISBETT, J. D. and ILLSLEY, R. 'The Influence of Early Puberty on Test Performance at the Age of Eleven.' *British Journal of Educational Psychology* (1963), **33**, p. 169.

PETERSON, A. D. C. 'Secondary Reorganisation in England and Wales.' *Comparative Education* (1965), **1**, p. 161.

PRINGLE, M. L. K., BUTLER, N. R. and DAVIE, R. *11,000 Seven-year-olds.* Longmans (1966).

ROGAN, E. *Report of the Bristol Medical Officer of Health* (1958), Appendix B.

RUTTER, M. *Children of Sick Parents.* Oxford University Press (1966).

SORSBY, A., SHERIDAN, M. and LEARY, G. A. *Refraction, and its Components in Twins.* (Medical Research Council Special Report Series No. 303.) Her Majesty's Stationery Office (1962).

TANNER, J. M. *Growth at Adolescence.* Blackwell, Oxford (1955).

UNESCO. *Educational Achievement of Thirteen-year-olds in Twelve Countries.* Institution for Education, Hamburg (1962).

WISEMAN, S. *Education and Environment.* Manchester University Press (1964).

[231]

PUBLICATIONS OF THE NATIONAL SURVEY

I. EDUCATION

1. Douglas, J. W. B. 'Waste of Talent.' *Advancement of Science*, March 1963, p. 564.
2. Douglas, J. W. B. *The Home and the School*. MacGibbon & Kee, 1964.
3. Douglas, J. W. B., and Ross, J. M. 'The Effects of Absence on Primary School Performance.' *The British Journal of Educational Psychology*, 1965, **35**, p. 28.
4. Douglas, J. W. B., and Ross, J. M. 'The Later Educational Progress and Emotional Adjustment of Children who went to Nursery Schools or Classes.' *Educational Research*, 1964, **7**, No. 1, p. 73.
5. Douglas, J. W. B., and Ross, J. M. 'Age of Puberty Related to Educational Ability, Attainment and School Leaving Age.' *Journal of Child Psychology and Psychiatry*, 1964, **5**, p. 185.
6. Douglas, J. W. B. 'Education and Social Movement.' In *Biological Aspects of Social Problems*. Edited by Meade and Parkes. Oliver & Boyd, 1965.
7. Douglas, J. W. B., Ross, J. M., and Simpson, H. R. 'Some Observations on the Relationships between Heights and Measured Ability among School Children.' *Human Biology*, 1965, **37**, p. 178.
8. Douglas, J. W. B., Ross, J. M., Walker, D. A., and Maxwell, S. M. 'Differences in Test Score and in the Gaining of Selective Places for Scottish Children and those in England and Wales.' *British Journal of Educational Psychology*, 1966, **36**, p. 150.
9. Ross, J. M., and Case, P. 'Why do Children Leave Grammar School Early?' *New Society*, 4th November 1965.
10. Douglas, J. W. B. 'The Age of Reaching Puberty: Some Associated Factors and Some Educational Implications.' *The Scientific Basis of Medicine Annual Reviews*, 1966, p. 91.
11. Ross, J. M., and Case, P. 'Who goes to Oxbridge?' *New Society*, 19th May 1966.
12. Douglas, J. W. B., and Ross, J. M. 'Single Sex or Co-ed? The Academic Consequences.' *Where*, May 1966.
13. Douglas, J. W. B. 'The School Progress of Nervous and Troublesome Children.' (Abstract) *British Journal of Psychiatry*, 1966, **112**, p. 1115.
14. Ross, J. M. 'Should More Grammar School Boys apply to Oxbridge.' *Where*, March 1967.

15. Douglas, J. W. B., Ross, J. M., and Cooper, J. E. 'The Relationship Between Handedness, Attainment and Adjustment in a National Sample of School Children.' *Educational Research*, 1967, **9**, p. 223.
16. Douglas, J. W. B., Ross, J. M., and Simpson, H. R. 'The Ability and Attainment of Short Sighted Pupils.' *Journal of the Royal Statistical Society*, Series A, 1967, **130**, p. 479.

II. BEHAVIOUR PROBLEMS

1. Bransby, E. R., Blomfield, J. M., and Douglas, J. W. B. 'The Prevalence of Bed-Wetting.' *Medical Officer*, 1955, **94**, p. 5.
2. Blomfield, J. M., and Douglas, J. W. B. 'Bed-wetting; Prevalence Among Children Aged 4–7 years.' *Lancet*, 1956, **1**, p. 850.
3. Douglas, J. W. B., and Mulligan, D. G. 'Emotional Adjustment and Educational Achievement—the Preliminary Results of a Longitudinal Study of a National Sample of Children.' *Proceedings of the Royal Society of Medicine*, 1961, **54**, p. 885.
4. Mulligan, D. G., Douglas, J. W. B., Hammond, W. A., and Tizard, J. 'Delinquency and Symptoms of Maladjustment; the Findings of a Longitudinal Study.' *Proceedings of the Royal Society of Medicine*, 1963, **56**, p. 1.
5. Douglas, J. W. B., Ross, J. M., Hammond, W. A., and Mulligan, D. G. 'Delinquency and Social Class.' *The British Journal of Criminology*, 1966, **6**, p. 294.
6. Mulligan, D. G. 'Some Correlates of Maladjustment in a National Sample of Schoolchildren.' Doctor of Philosophy Thesis (Faculty of Arts), University of London, 1964.

III. ILLNESS

1. Douglas, J. W. B. 'Social Class Differences in Health and Survival during the First Two Years of Life; the Results of a National Survey.' *Population Studies*, 1951, **5**, p. 35.
2. Douglas, J. W. B. 'The Health and Survival of Children in Different Social Classes; the Results of a National Survey.' *Lancet*, 1951, **2**, p. 440.
3. Rowntree, G. 'Accidents Among Children under Two Years of Age in Great Britain.' *Journal of Hygiene*, 1950, **48**, p. 323.
4. Rowntree, G. 'Accidents Among Children.' *Monthly Bulletin of the Ministry of Health*, 1951, **10**, p. 150.
5. Blomfield, J. M. 'An Account of Hospital Admissions in the Pre-School Period.' Mimeographed—copies available on application to the Joint Committee.
6. Douglas, J. W. B. 'Ability and Adjustment of Children who have had Measles.' *British Medical Journal*, 1964, **2**, p. 1301.

[233]

7. Cooper, J. E. 'Epilepsy and a Longitudinal Survey of 5,000 Children.' *British Medical Journal*, 1965, **1**, p. 1020.
8. Douglas, J. W. B., and Waller, R. E. 'Air Pollution and Respiratory Infection in Children.' *British Journal of Preventive and Social Medicine*, 1966, **20**, p. 1.

IV. THE PREMATURE CHILD

1. Douglas, J. W. B. 'Some Factors Associated with Prematurity.' *Journal of Obstetrics and Gynaecology of the British Empire*, 1950, **57**, p. 625.
2. Douglas, J. W. B. 'Birthweight and the History of Breast-feeding.' *Lancet*, 1954, **ii**, p. 685.
3. Douglas, J. W. B., and Mogford, C. 'The Health of Premature Children During the First Four Years of Life.' *British Medical Journal*, 1953, **1**, p. 748.
4. Douglas, J. W. B., and Mogford, C. 'The Growth of Premature Children.' *Archives of Disease in Childhood*, 1953, **28**, p. 436.
5. Douglas, J. W. B. 'The Age at which Premature Children Walk.' *Medical Officer*, 1956, **95**, p. 33.
6. Douglas, J. W. B. 'The Mental Ability of Premature Children.' *British Medical Journal*, 1956, **1**, p. 1210.
7. Douglas, J. W. B. 'Premature Children at Primary Schools.' *British Medical Journal*, 1960, **1**, p. 1008.

V. THE MATERNITY AND CHILD WELFARE SERVICES

1. 'A Survey of Childbearing in Britain.' *Population Studies*, 1947, **1**, p. 99.
2. *Maternity in Great Britain*. Oxford University Press, 1948.
3. Douglas, J. W. B., and Rowntree, G. 'Supplementary Maternal and Child Health Services. Part I, Postnatal Care—Part II, Nurseries.' *Population Studies*, 1949, **3**, p. 205.
4. Rowntree, G. 'Supplementary Child Health Services. Part III, Infant Welfare Centres.' *Population Studies*, 1950, **3**, p. 375.
5. Rowntree, G. 'Diptheria Immunization in a National Sample of Children Aged Two Years in March 1948.' *Monthly Bulletin of the Ministry of Health*, 1950, **9**, p. 134.
6. Douglas, J. W. B. 'Deux Enquêtes Nationales sur la Maternité et la Santé de l'Enfant en Grande Bretagne.' *Population*, 1950, **5**, p. 625.
7. Douglas, J. W. B. 'The Environmental Challenge in Early Childhood.' *Public Health*, **78**, p. 195.

VI. MISCELLANEOUS

1. Douglas, J. W. B. 'The Extent of Breast-Feeding in Great Britain in 1946, with Special Reference to the Health and Survival of Children.'

[234]

Journal of Obstetrics and Gynaecology of the British Empire, 1950, **57**, p. 336.

2. MacCarthy, D., Douglas, J. W. B., and Mogford, C. 'Circumcision in a National Sample of Four-Year-Old Children.' *British Medical Journal*, 1952, **2**, p. 755.

3. Rowntree, G. 'Early Childhood in Broken Families.' *Population Studies*, 1955, **8**, p. 247.

4. Douglas, J. W. B., and Blomfield, J. M. 'Maternal Employment and the Welfare of Children—an Account of a Survey in Progress.' *Eugenics Review*, 1957, **49**, p. 69.

5. Douglas, J. W. B., and Blomfield, J. M. *Children Under Five.* Allen & Unwin Ltd, 1958.

6. Douglas, J. W. B., and Simpson, H. R. 'Height in Relation to Puberty, Family Size and Social Class: a longitudinal study.' *Milbank Memorial Fund Quarterly*, 1964, **42**, p. 20.

7. Nelson, D. M. 'Studying the Employment and Training of a National Sample of 17-year-olds.' *Occupational Psychology*, 1964, **38**, p. 183.

8. Douglas, J. W. B., and Blomfield, J. M. 'The Reliability of Longitudinal Surveys.' *Milbank Memorial Fund Quarterly*, 1956, **34**, p. 227.

Index

Absence from School, 85, 93, 112, 113, 114, 121, 157, 162–8, 171, 181, 191
Accidents, 111
Achievement, over-and-under, 21–2, 39–40, 44–5, 47, 88–89, 100–1, 105–6, 111, 113, 114, 115, 122, 126, 130, 158–9, 160, 166, 173, 191, 193
Adjustment, 103–4, 107–16, 121, 122–3, 131, 147, 151, 178, 181, 189
  See also Teachers, ratings and assessments of Pupils
Adolescence, 31, 135–44, 157, 160, 163, 190–1
  classification of, 137, 200
Aggressiveness
  See Adjustment
Apprenticeships, 24
Approved Schools, 23
Aspirations of Pupils
  for further education, 27, 31, 63, 71, 76, 77, 130, 131, 159, 160
  for future employment, 31, 98–101, 105, 160, 181
Attendance at School
  See Absence from School
Attitude to Work, 37, 85, 93, 103–6, 107, 111–14, 118, 120–1, 131, 133, 156, 157, 160, 164, 171, 173, 178, 180, 181

Behaviour
  See Teachers, ratings and assessments of Pupils; Adjustment
Bernstein, B., 127
Binet, A., 107
Birth
  order, 129–32, 142
  spacing, 132–4, 139, 142
  weight, 139
  See also Family size

Bonham, D. G., xii
Borderline Pupils, definition of, 192
Broken Homes
  See Parents—death, separation and divorce
Brown, B., 87
Boys
  progress compared with girls, 29–34
  See also subject headings
Burt, C., 147, 148, 149
Butler, N. R., xii, 6
Bytheway, B., 21

Central Advisory Council for Education, xii, 23, 38, 73, 127
Certificate of Secondary Education, 26, 46
Child Guidance Clinics, 110
Circular 10/65, 59
Co-education, 33, 66–73, 144, 179, 188
Cohort Studies, xiii, xiv, 6
Comer, D., 155
Committee on Higher Education, xii
Comprehensive System and Schools, 5, 6, 28, 58–65
Crowther Report
  See Central Advisory Council for Education

Dale, R. R., 67, 72
Dancy, J., 53, 54
Davie, R., 6
Delinquents, 110, 114, 115, 117–23, 181, 189
Department of Education and Science, 59, 77, 135, 197
Deutsch, M., 87
Douglas, J. W. B., 119, 138, 163
  See also *Home and the School, The*

[237]

[239]

Urban Areas, 44, 69, 181

Verbal Stimulation, 126–7
Vernon, P. E., 195

Wiseman, S., 19, 45

Younger or Youngest
    See Birth order; Family size